joyful momentum

"Christian friendship is a gift that no woman should be without. In *Joyful Momentum*, Elizabeth Tomlin gives us an avenue for making that possible, offering practical and concrete examples of how friendship can be nurtured through the development of women's ministries that reach out to those who are hungry for a deeper connection with their sisters."

Ann Garrido
Associate professor of homiletics at
the Aquinas Institute of Theology
Author of *Redeeming Conflict*

"With powerful, practical, and spirit-filled writing, Elizabeth Tomlin builds upon foundational concepts for starting, maintaining, and growing an effective, faith-filled women's ministry, and more importantly, leading women into a deep and lasting relationship with Jesus Christ. I highly recommend this thorough and well-written guide!"

Michele Faehnle
Codirector of the Columbus Catholic Women's Conference
Coauthor of *The Friendship Project*

"*Joyful Momentum* offers a perfect blend of tangible examples, faith-filled wisdom, and organizational insight; Elizabeth Tomlin has developed a foundational resource for reviving and sustaining women's ministry. Every parish needs this book."

Samantha Povlock
Founder and director of FemCatholic

"*Joyful Momentum* should be required reading for every women's ministry team: not only for its practical tips but also because going through it together will help to form the kind of team and ministry that bears lasting fruit. With wisdom grown from experience, Tomlin roots her vision of women's ministry in our Christian vocation and God-given feminine gifts. She draws helpful strategies from scripture and the saints, encourages groups to draw strength from and give back to parish life, and offers a merciful approach to conflict resolution. Any women's ministry founded on the principles and practices shared in this book is bound to build 'joyful momentum' and bear lasting fruit."

Sarah Christmyer
Codeveloper and founding editor of
The Great Adventure Catholic Bible study
Author of *Becoming Women of the Word*

"*Joyful Momentum* both explains why women's ministry is so critically important in today's Church and shows how you can grow a thriving women's faith community in your parish. Whether you are building from the ground up or are part of an established group looking to take your ministry to the next level, you'll learn from Elizabeth's personal experience in establishing and leading ministries around the country. Trust her as a guide and joyful companion to creating the greatest gift you can give yourself and your parish!"

Lisa M. Hendey
Founder of CatholicMom.com

"*Joyful Momentum* is the go-to handbook for today's Catholic women's ministries. Through heartfelt and inspiring anecdotes, Tomlin shows the reader how to discern the call to women's ministry and offers the fundamental how-tos of building it. Essential foundational elements and unsurpassed practices are underscored as abundant encouragement is woven throughout to help you to discover your feminine genius; to know, love, and serve God through women's ministry. Tomlin also shows how to keep a joyful momentum, avoid discouragement, competition, and conflict. I highly recommend this book!"

Donna-Marie Cooper O'Boyle
EWTN host and author of *Rooted in Love*

joyful momentum

GROWING AND SUSTAINING VIBRANT WOMEN'S GROUPS

A CATHOLIC HANDBOOK

ELIZABETH A. TOMLIN

AVE MARIA PRESS AVE Notre Dame, Indiana

Imprimatur Archbishop Timothy P. Broglio
            Archdiocese for the Military Services, USA
            August 16, 2019

Founded in 1865, Ave Maria Press is a ministry of the United States Province of Holy Cross.

www.avemariapress.com

Paperback: ISBN-13 978-1-59471-943-1

E-book: ISBN-13 978-1-59471-944-8

Cover image © seb_ra/Getty Images.

Cover and text design by Brianna Dombo.

Printed and bound in the United States of America.

Library of Congress Cataloging-in-Publication Data
Names: Tomlin, Elizabeth A., author.
Title: Joyful momentum : growing and sustaining vibrant women's groups / Elizabeth A. Tomlin.
Description: Notre Dame, Indiana : Ave Maria Press, 2020. | "A Catholic handbook." | Summary: "In Joyful Momentum, Elizabeth Tomlin shows readers how they can start, expand, strengthen, or retool an existing women's group or ministry in their own Catholic parish"--Provided by publisher.
Identifiers: LCCN 2019046027 (print) | LCCN 2019046028 (ebook) | ISBN 9781594719431 (paperback) | ISBN 9781594719448 (ebook)
Subjects: LCSH: Church work with women--Catholic Church. | Church group work--Catholic Church. | Church group work with women. | Small groups--Religious aspects--Catholic Church.
Classification: LCC BX2347.8.W6 T665 2020 (print) | LCC BX2347.8.W6 (ebook) | DDC 259.082--dc23
LC record available at https://lccn.loc.gov/2019046027
LC ebook record available at https://lccn.loc.gov/2019046028

FOR MY FAMILY

MY HUSBAND, GREGORY,
AND OUR CHILDREN,
PATRICK, HANNAH, AND
GEORGE MONROE

FOR MY SISTERS IN CHRIST
IN THE MILITARY COUNCIL OF
CATHOLIC WOMEN

MAY WE ALWAYS
"ROUSE ONE ANOTHER TO
LOVE AND GOOD WORKS"
(HEB 10:24)

contents

Introduction:

THEY SHARED ALL THINGS IN COMMON

> They devoted themselves to the teaching of the apostles and to the communal life, to the breaking of the bread and to the prayers.
>
> —Acts 2:42

"Mom, I'm hurt! I fell off my sled, and my arm really hurts!" These tearful words echoed over my cell phone from my thirteen-year-old son, Patrick, as I drove my nine-year-old daughter, Hannah, home from her weekly violin lesson. As I wound my Ford Explorer through the mountains surrounding our home in the Hudson Highlands at the US Army garrison at West Point, New York, the cell-phone signal was fleeting, but as best I could, I harnessed calm and instructed Patrick to go into the house, put a bag of frozen peas on his arm, and watch TV until I returned home in five minutes.

In reality, those five minutes were about forty minutes because I could not get back to the house until I picked up my fourteen-month-old baby, George, from day care. Upon arriving home, I found that Patrick had followed directions, but he was huddled in a fetal position, whimpering in pain. With one look at his contorted arm I thought, "Wow! That. Is. Not. Normal. Arms are not supposed to do that!" To keep Patrick from getting hysterical, I took a breath, whispered a prayer, and said in my most prescriptively metered tone, "Okay, buddy. It looks like you broke your arm. Let's get you to the hospital."

The kids climbed back into the Explorer, and we retraced the path down the mountain toward the army hospital to embark upon our evening in the emergency room. Since my mental state was in response mode for Patrick's immediate need for medical care, I did not think through the facts that it was dinnertime, none of the kids had eaten, and the $1.25 in change in my wallet would barely buy a bag of Doritos from the vending machine.

Within an hour, Patrick was taken for x-rays, Hannah was bored and hungry, and George was lying on the floor of the emergency room crying for food. These chaotic days were when I missed my husband, Greg, the most. You see, our family was navigating a situation intimately familiar to many military families: Greg was serving month seven of a twelve-month deployment. While I knew his heart was with us, there was no way for him to help us physically that evening.

I started to feel defeated but then remembered something. A good friend, Nicole, whom I met through the women's ministry group at the Catholic chapel, had leaned over the pew multiple times to say, "Elizabeth, if you ever need anything, please call. I mean it." Despite her heartfelt offer of hospitality, I had privately resolved not to ask for help during this year. Rather stubbornly, I told myself that I was strong and could manage on my own.

But that is not the point of being in community with others. In Christian charity, my friend offered to help, and I was being pretty uncharitable in refusing to let her, or anyone else, help me. This day, however, was different. I needed help! I retrieved my cell phone and called my friend. When she answered, I said in a weak voice, "Nicole?" "Elizabeth?" she responded. I managed to say, "I need help . . ."

I don't remember the rest of the conversation, but within five minutes, Nicole, brimming with energy, appeared at the sliding-glass emergency-room doors pushing a double jogging stroller loaded up with blankets. She had walked to the hospital from her house in the stinging cold of that February night! Without any pretenses, Nicole got to work. She buckled baby George into the stroller and covered him snugly. She assured me to take my time with Patrick and that she would take care of Hannah and George.

Patrick and I spent the next few hours snacking on cheese-flavored Doritos—thanks to that $1.25 in change—as we drew tic-tac-toe and hangman games on the paper gurney sheet, and eventually had his arm set in a cast. After Patrick was discharged, we drove the short distance to Nicole's house to pick up the younger children.

When I entered the dimly lit living room, I found Nicole's husband rocking in a chair with George sound asleep on his chest. My pulse stopped for a second or two. For months, George had not been rocked to sleep by his father, but this night he was fast asleep in the arms of a father who was enjoying rocking a baby as much as George enjoyed being rocked. I was overwhelmed. It was the sweetest thing I had seen in some time. I thanked Nicole for her kindness and wearily but gratefully took the kids home.

God showed me that evening one aspect of why women's ministry is important and necessary in a vibrant Catholic community. In a tense situation, God made himself known to me through a friendship built in our parish women's ministry. God reveals himself in a variety of ways. In John's gospel, Mary Magdalene recognizes her resurrected Lord when he calls her name (see John 20:16). We learn from Luke's gospel that the men on the road to Emmaus recognize Jesus in the breaking of the bread: "And it happened that, while he was with them at table, he took bread, said the blessing, broke it, and gave it to them. With that their eyes were opened and they recognized him" (Lk 24:30–31). God incarnate may have revealed himself to Mary through speech and to the men going to Emmaus through bread, but that

February night God showed his love incarnate for my family through a friend with a double stroller and a father rocking my sleeping baby.

I did not realize it until later, but the foundation for this manifestation of God's love had been prepared through intentional, everyday interactions between Nicole and me in the women's ministry group at our Catholic chapel. Over shared Mass attendance, spiritual reading, strong coffee, carbohydrate-laden potluck breakfast casseroles, praying the Rosary, visiting a nursing home for retired nuns, decorating the church for Christmas, and even weeding the church garden, we had forged a kinship mediated by Christ's love.

LET'S GET ACQUAINTED

But let's back up. How is it that you came to be reading a book about women's ministry written by me, a person who believes with as much certainty as I believe in gravity that women's ministry is essential to vibrant parish life and the propagation of the faith? Maybe you have been asking God to help you meet other Catholic women at your parish, but you don't see a natural opportunity that fits with your schedule. Or perhaps you're interested in a certain book or service opportunity, and you would like to share that experience with others in your parish. Or maybe you tried the current offerings at your parish, and they don't quite fit your needs. Don't worry—this book will help!

I have been involved in women's ministry in some capacity for most of my adult life. The first time I attended a women's ministry was my sophomore year in college. My bestie, Melissa, invited me. So, I went. I was curious but not expecting anything. About six of us gathered in a small circle on the floor of a college residence-hall kitchen. When the group leader asked us to open our Bibles to the Gospel of John, I opened my Bible to the *First Letter* (epistle) of John. Though a cradle Catholic and raised going to Mass on Sundays, I had a hard time navigating the scriptures on my own.

The leader asked me to read a verse, and I did, but it was from the wrong book—and I was mortified. The leader graciously helped me find the right passage and correct course. Then something happened: I discovered that I loved what we were learning. I came back to the group week after week, eager to learn more. I wanted to learn about the faith as well as the women who shared their lives with me. What's more, I wanted to follow their example.

After college, which included some graduate work in theology, I gradually started taking more active leadership roles in women's ministries. (Please note that while formal theological training can be useful, especially for catechists and teachers, you certainly don't need a degree to serve the Church with your gifts!)

During our years at West Point, I came to know the Archdiocese for the Military Services, USA, and its women's ministry group, the Military Council of Catholic Women (MCCW). This was where I met Nicole, my emergency-room rescuer.

In 2012, I helped organize the MCCW as a nonprofit, directed MCCW's faith-formation program from 2012 to 2014, and served as the president of the MCCW from 2014 to 2016. Since then I have continued to serve in this ministry, helping it extend its reach to even more women through our shared faith. Today, the MCCW forms a faith community of Catholic women across the United States and across the world. Local groups gather regularly for faith studies and fellowship, and throughout the year we hold several faith-formation retreats and conferences in the United States, Europe, and Asia.[1] It has been a privilege to see how God has made this ministry grow through the good work of many faithful women.

Now, before you are tempted to close this book, overwhelmed at the thought of God calling you to do something this complex, please keep reading. I assure you that this is far more about God's grace than my natural abilities. If someone had asked eighteen-year-old, college-aged me—the woman who did not know the difference between the First Letter of John and the Gospel of John—if I would someday lead a women's ministry for a global archdiocese, the answer would have been a resounding, "No way. I'm not smart enough. I don't know enough. I'm too sinful. I'm not good enough."

And if I had done that, I would have fallen into a trap of deceit set by the enemy of our souls, who wants us to doubt our God-given potential and believe that we are not good enough to know and serve a God who wants nothing more than our love.

However, by God's grace, I am good enough. You are good enough. In fact, we are "very good" (Gn 1:31). God does not expect us to be perfect in our women's ministry work; he asks for our obedience to his calling. God puts that burning restlessness in our spirits that propels us to seek something outside our own comfort zones, that causes us to want to draw close to Christ, and that makes us want to connect with other women in our faith walks. I am grateful that God put in my heart a curiosity to know him and love him, and a spirit to serve him.

WHY WOMEN'S MINISTRY?

Other than that college Bible study, my women's ministry experience has predominantly been in military communities, where we know that the work of the service member is inherently dangerous, and families are often separated because of deployments and extensive training time in the field or at sea. Women's ministry becomes the foundation of a necessary network of support in which the proverbial "village" that raises children is a trustworthy one that shares values and life experiences.

However, the same is true about any vital, sustainable women's ministry outside military life—participants rely on one another, trust one another, and grow in the cardinal virtues of faith, hope, and love together in authentic spiritual friendship.

Throughout the New Testament, the closest Greek word to describe the intimate relationships formed through women's ministry is *koinonia*. "They devoted themselves to the teaching of the apostles and to the communal life (*koinonia*), to the breaking of the bread and to the prayers" (Acts 2:42). For me, the *koinonia* forged in women's ministry goes beyond mere "communal life"; it is the enduring fruit of devoted friendship, catechesis, and prayer, undergirded by the love of Christ. We foster a communal life of faith and friendship through catechesis, prayer, and participating in the sacraments.

Women's ministry is important because it invites us to a venue to learn about the Christian faith and live it in ways that befit the feminine genius with which God uniquely endows each of us.[2]

Women's ministry can be surprising, humorous, and yes, even frustrating at times, but that can be overcome with a lot of cooperation and ingenuity. St. Teresa of Ávila reflected that "men of learning seem to get theology without much effort. But we women need to take it all in slowly and muse on it. We need to feel it."[3] And as we take the time to talk about it and bond over it, we discover another aspect of the feminine genius, as new life emerges from those moments of shared generosity, compassion, intuition, and vulnerability.

Could anyone have met me at the emergency room on that chaotic night? Yes. We know that there are good Samaritans in this world. But my relationship with Nicole that night was special. It was *koinonia*. Nicole's help was living the communal life and sharing Christ's love. Our shared relationship, mediated in the Church, inspired her to offer assistance and moved me to ask for help. This shared relationship in the Church sustains our friendship to this day.

HOW TO USE THIS BOOK

As you are reading this book, maybe something is stirring within you. Perhaps you have a hunger to find a friend like Nicole. Maybe someone like Melissa invited you to a gathering and you simply accepted her invitation to help create a new ministry. If so, welcome!

People venture into leadership roles for all kinds of reasons. Perhaps you are consulting this book to begin a new women's ministry, or you are formulating a plan to help you strengthen an existing ministry. Maybe you feel disheartened or unappreciated in your current ministry and you are ready for something new. You know that women's ministry is important, but you are not sure where God is calling you now. No matter where you are in your life in women's ministry, my hope is that *Joyful Momentum* will help you reflect on your work more deeply and provide tools and best practices to keep moving forward.

momentum builders
TIPS FOR GETTING STARTED

Tip #1. Move forward with a team. If a women's ministry has not yet been established in your community, seek out other women who may feel called to start one. Make an announcement at Mass; put an invitation in the bulletin and on the church's social media, inviting women to an interest meeting so that many hands can assist in starting the ministry. The initial gathering does not have to be large, but we know that God sends us out at least two by two, so do your best.

Tip #2. Let this book serve as a guide to starting or revitalizing a women's ministry. Use *Joyful Momentum* as a group study to share experiences of ministry, celebrate your good work, and consider how the ministry could be strengthened through applying the practices and strategies shared in each chapter. Be prepared for God to work through you, and enjoy the surprises along the way!

Tip #3. A vibrant women's ministry benefits the entire faith community. Women's ministry provides an environment in which women grow in faith (through catechesis), hope (through prayer and sacrament), and love (through shared relationships). And yet the benefits extend to the rest of the community as well. Through vibrant women's ministries I have witnessed women returning to the Church and communities growing outwardly in missionary discipleship. Parishes that invest in women's ministry often see corresponding growth in other areas: members of the group may be more likely to enroll their children in religious-education programs, have their marriages convalidated and their children baptized, and influence their non-Catholic spouses to enroll in RCIA. When women's ministry thrives, the whole parish benefits.

You have taken a step to responding to that restlessness that God has placed within you to work in women's ministry. However, no one can do ministry alone. Women's ministry is by definition relational, and so this book will show you how to gather your "tribe" and make plans as a group.

Joyful Momentum has eight chapters, and each explores a different facet of women's ministry. The first two chapters are foundational: Chapter 1 explores two kinds of Christ-centered relationships that are vital to any woman's ministry: friend-to-friend (within the team) and team-to-pastor (within the parish). Chapter 2 presents women's ministry as a vocation—a call within a call. It invites readers into a process of discernment about their vocation in women's ministry.

The remaining chapters of *Joyful Momentum* offer a practical guidebook to *doing* the work of women's ministry and include many ideas, exercises, and best practices. These chapters incorporate essential elements of women's ministry:

- Learn how to practice hospitality that attracts women currently sitting in your pews who have never attended a women's ministry, and to go outside the comfort zone of your parish to introduce women around you to Jesus.
- Rediscover (or discover for the first time) the spiritual gifts that God has given you to build up your faith community.
- Build a team that celebrates one another's spiritual gifts and diversities and avoids traps of comparison and insecurity.
- Assess the efforts of your group and make changes in ways that unify people.
- Offer and seek forgiveness when conflicts arise in relationships—and understand when to walk away from toxic relationships when they hinder your ability to do the work God calls you to do.
- Find out how to pass the leadership baton without losing momentum and how to find (and be) spiritual mentors.

Each chapter is structured in three parts: *Share*, *Apply*, and *Ponder*.

Share. Women naturally relate to one another through sharing our experiences, feelings, and dreams. We lift up one another through listening empathetically, offering encouraging words, expressing our love for one another through our deeds, supporting one another in prayer, and just holding a hand or sharing a hug. The Share section of each chapter does exactly that—it shares personal experiences in women's ministry that relate to the theme of each chapter.

Apply. The second part of each chapter invites readers to reflect upon an essential element of women's ministry theologically through scripture and Church teaching. This section presents aspects of the lives and writings of women saints such as Teresa of Ávila, Teresa of Calcutta, Elizabeth Ann Seton, Thérèse of Lisieux, Katharine Drexel, Faustina Kowalska, Hildegard of Bingen, and Blessed Jutta of Disibodenberg. These women loved God and their neighbors. They were passionate about the faith, practical, witty, and diversely gifted. They provide a compelling witness of discipleship for women's ministry and, indeed, for the whole Church.

Each *Apply* section incorporates a feature called "Momentum Builders" containing tips, exercises for group discussion, and other how-tos that can be adapted to a wide variety of groups and ministries. Additional online, printable resources are available at joyfulmomentum.org or avemariapress.com.

Ponder. Each chapter concludes with scripture passages and questions to use, individually or as a group, to help you apply the material to your particular circumstances and ministry goals.

St. Teresa of Ávila taught that "God appreciates it when we do not put limits on his work."[4] God will work wonders with a team that is open to the promptings of the Holy Spirit. I dare say that with an active and healthy women's ministry *koinonia*, parishes and indeed the world can be transformed. Let's get started.

PONDER

Today's passage to ponder is from Acts 2:42–47:

> They devoted themselves to the teaching of the apostles and to the communal life, to the breaking of the bread and to the prayers. Awe came upon everyone, and many wonders and signs were done through the apostles. All who believed were together and had all things in common; they would sell their property and

possessions and divide them among all according to each one's need. Every day they devoted themselves to meeting together in the temple area and to breaking bread in their homes. They ate their meals with exultation and sincerity of heart, praising God and enjoying favor with all the people. And every day the Lord added to their number those who were being saved.

1. This passage describes the nascent Church in Jerusalem. How does this community resemble the Church today? How can our parishes more closely strive for this community?
2. Think of a woman who has helped you grow in your relationship with Jesus. How did this person encourage, instruct, or model the faith for you?
3. Do you help other women grow in their faith? If so, how do you share your faith with them?
4. Have you ever participated in a women's ministry? If so, describe your favorite experience in women's ministry. How did this experience resemble the Acts 2 community? How did this community enhance your life and the life of the parish?
5. Have you ever experienced the gift of receiving from a "Nicole" in your own life? In what way can you extend Christian charity to someone else today? Do it.

1

Foundational Relationships:

THE FAVOR OF SPIRITUAL FRIENDSHIP

What a good favor God does to those he places in the company of good people!
—St. Teresa of Ávila

SHARE

Do you have a best friend? I have always been friendly with many people, but few people know the inner workings of my heart—my prayers, aspirations, insecurities, and the places in which God is challenging me or allowing me to struggle.

My friend Maggie is one of these precious people. We met through the army while our husbands were stationed in Fort Bliss, Texas. We bonded over a conversation about Mary because, when we met, we were both wearing necklaces with medals of Mary. We share many things in common, including our goofy personalities, the adventure of raising young children, and army life. In Texas, we met weekly for a Bible study, shared our

Thanksgiving tables, cared for each other's children, and confided in each other about nearly everything. There are few areas in my life in which Maggie has not offered support or counsel. The thread that ties our experiences together is our Catholic faith. We point each other toward Christ and help each other when we falter.

Several years ago, Maggie and I were fortunate to spend a weekend together in San Diego, California, at a Catholic women's ministry gathering. During the opening dinner at an Italian restaurant, I ordered a glass of chianti, and I noticed that Maggie ordered lemonade. Knowing that Maggie enjoys a peppery chianti as much as I do, I stared at her with a look of "Do you have something to tell me?" She returned my raised eyebrows with a smirk of "Yes, I have something to tell you."

Maggie shared with our gathering that she was pregnant, and we all cheered at this announcement. In contrast to her previous two pregnancies, Maggie was seven weeks along and relieved that she was not in the throes of morning sickness. In fact, she felt great. One of our many bonding points is that we are both violently nauseous in the early stages of pregnancy. My four miscarriages each followed weeks of not feeling sick enough. Knowing Maggie's similarly queasy history, I made a cautious mental note.

After dinner, we returned to our hotel rooms, and about fifteen minutes later, my phone rang. Sobs poured through the receiver, and I instantly knew what had happened. I grabbed my pajamas and toothbrush and said to my roommate, "I won't be back tonight, but pray for Maggie. She's having a miscarriage."

I stayed with Maggie that night. We prayed for her, the family, and the baby, and we cried and laughed through all the emotions women have when we lose a baby. With mascara smeared down her face, Maggie remarked that if she had to go through this with someone other than her husband, she was glad it was with me.

The next morning, I found our group leader and explained what happened. Our gathering met for morning Mass, and afterward, our priest, Fr. Joe, called us into a circle at the front of the church. He reflected on a verse from the book of Job: "The LORD gave and the LORD has taken away; blessed be the name of the LORD!" (1:21). "Oh yeah? Where is the blessing?" some of us wondered. Our priest showed us. Fr. Joe anointed Maggie with the Sacrament of Anointing of the Sick, for healing—for her body and her broken heart. Then he offered to anoint any other woman who felt the need for healing from losing a baby. Of the forty women, at least twenty-five came forward to receive an anointing. Through this experience we were blessed with sacramental grace and grew closer by sharing about the children we will not meet on this side of heaven.

So often women hold losses like this privately in our hearts. The first time I miscarried, I spent Sunday after Sunday sitting in the back row of the church with tears welling up in my eyes. I told myself that if I did not blink, the tears could not spill out all over the hymnal, so I would not, *technically speaking*, be crying in public. This was, of course, nonsense. The tears always spilled.

Our society does not love our unborn children the way we do, and our neighbors or coworkers may not grasp the magnitude of pain that a miscarriage can bring. However, because my friendship with Maggie is a Christ-centered, spiritual friendship, we traversed the valley of tears vulnerably with each other, turning to God through prayer with our community, being fortified by the Eucharist and the grace of the Sacrament of Anointing of the Sick. With Fr. Joe's pastoral care, we rightfully put this sad experience into God's hands.

APPLY
FOUNDATIONAL RELATIONSHIPS

This experience highlights two types of foundational relationships in women's ministry. First, a women's ministry is built upon Christ-centered relationships that may develop into spiritual friendships. Second, a women's ministry must cultivate a relationship with the pastor who provides necessary shepherd's care and makes available the graces of the sacraments. A ministry may begin with friendships between women who meet for Bible study over coffee, or the pastor may ask women who do not know each other to join together and start ministry. Whatever the origin, without both spiritual friendships and pastoral care, a Catholic women's ministry cannot be.

Getting Started

If God is calling you to start a women's ministry from scratch or build an existing ministry, gather Christ-centered women by casting a wide net. Make an invitation at Mass. Put an announcement in the church bulletin or on social media. Extend invitations through your personal network inside and outside the parish. Schedule a time to meet with all women who are interested, as well at the priest, to collaborate. With a few Christ-centered friendships and pastoral care, you have a ministry.

But what are Christ-centered friends, and how do you find them—and where do you begin if you want to connect with your busy pastor? Let's talk about that now.

Cultivate Spiritual Friendships

In spiritual (or Christ-centered) friendships, people desire what is truly good for each other, and they point each other toward union with God. In *Love and Responsibility*, Pope John Paul II describes that friendship, and later, love, develop from sympathy. The word *sympathy* has two Greek roots: *syn* (with) and the root of the verb *pathein* (to experience). To have sympathy is to experience *with* someone.[1]

Pope John Paul II uses the word *sympathy* to explain the development of both marital love and spiritual friendship. He explains that as people share experiences, their relationship can stagnate or it can grow into friendship.[2]

St. Teresa of Ávila describes desiring the good for another person as developing a "spiritual love" that must be practiced and perfected. She advises that we should cultivate spiritual friendships with virtuous people because when we see virtue in another, we desire that virtue in our lives. A good way to be close to God, she explains, "is to speak with his friends."[3]

According to St. Teresa, spiritual friends offer sincere counsel and correction. If one friend sees another deviate from virtue, she is compelled to tell her friend about it out of love, not condemnation. Spiritual friendships run deep. They do not flatter, envy, or gossip. They help us avoid, rather than feed, our own vices and weaknesses. Spiritual friends imitate the sacrificial love that Jesus has for us and embrace hardship without hesitation.

Spiritual friends, like mother-and-son saints Monica and Augustine, walk toward the same goal—unity with God. St. Teresa's spiritual friends, or "spiritual lovers," as she referred to them, were instrumental in her faith. "After the Lord," she remarked, "it is because of persons like these that I am not in hell; for I was always very attached to their praying for me, and so I strove to get them to do this."[4]

If you have Christ-centered friendships or spiritual friends, treasure them! They are transformational. Unfortunately our culture places a premium on the quantity of our interactions rather than the quality. Society obsesses over the amount of "likes," "shares," and "retweets" on social media. We exalt posts for being "viral" rather than virtuous. We share ephemeral "stories" that disappear in twenty-four hours rather than sharing *sympathy—* shared experiences. In this environment, spiritual friendships are countercultural. My daughter sometimes ask me, "Did you LMR?" That's teen for "Did you *like my recent* (social media post)?" To which I tell her, "No. ILYIP!"—I like you in person.

In contrast, spiritual friends seek *quality* over quantity; *virtue* over viral. Spiritual friends don't just like "your recent"; they love you always. In fact, most of the people we interact with regularly are not friends at all. It is difficult to have more than a few spiritual friends. We can love all people with Christian charity, but to make spiritual friends, we have to seek them out and invest time and emotion into cultivating these friendships. We have to give to these friends generously without expecting anything in return.

Women's ministry is inherently relational. To build a women's ministry, we need Christ-centered relationships that may develop into spiritual friendships, as we invest in them over time. It can be distressing to realize, in the process of cultivating spiritual friendships, that some of our "friendships" are not actual friendships. Some "friends" may be really fun or exceptionally comforting, but when we take a discerning look we realize that some people tempt or lure us away from virtue.

Do you have a "friend" who allows you to slink into gossip or caustic criticism of others? Maybe you have a friend with whom social drinking becomes social *drunking*. Do you have a "friend" who habitually uses you, puts you down, or kicks up a tornado of drama over the minutest disagreements? In her book *Good Enough Is Good Enough: Confessions of an Imperfect Catholic Mom*, my friend and fellow author Colleen Duggan confesses about her youth, "I sometimes tolerated friends who treated me poorly because it was easier to tolerate their poor behavior than the loneliness I sometimes felt."[5]

My friends, your deserve beautiful friends! Contemporary Swiss theologian Hans Urs von Balthasar spoke of truth and goodness as the sisters of beauty.[6] Beautiful—*spiritual*—friends will embody truth and goodness. Do not resign to ugly friendships. If you realize that some of your "friends" are not good friends, back away. Though backing away may make you feel lonely at first, you are doing yourself a great kindness, because this creates the time and emotional room to pursue spiritual friendships. If you decide to back away from a friendship, do so quietly, gently, and without gossip. St. Teresa of Ávila guided her community to retreat from poor relationships delicately. After all, since modeling virtue inspires virtue, your movement toward Christ may inspire someone else's.

Create a Circle of Friends

Pay attention to the people God brings across your path, and cultivate a circle of friends from within your parish as well as outside it. While not all of our friends have to be Catholic, looking for friends in your own parish is a great way to start to make spiritual friends.

There are a number of ways to meet people in the parish:

Go to Mass and say hello. Greet the person next to you in the pew. Notice the women who sit alone. My friend Rosalie's husband is Baptist. They are raising their children in the Catholic Church, but Rosalie's husband does not routinely attend Mass with his family. Rosalie has made a habit of looking for moms and kids in church without a dad present. Through this, she has cultivated Christ-centered relationships with other moms who encourage each other during Mass and pitch in whenever a small child needs extra attention.

Be active in the parish. If your parish has a breakfast or parish picnic, go! Go a step further and help with the next event. Consider teaching (or assisting with) religious education—many women of faith gravitate toward teaching. Perhaps there is a Bible study or existing women's ministry, an opportunity to feed the hungry, or a prayer ministry that piques your interest. If you are a parent, consider enrolling your children in a parochial school (if your budget permits), or affiliate with a parish scout troop. A Catholic Youth Organization sports team is a great way to plug into the community and meet mom friends on the sidelines.

Always leave room for one more. Actively draw newcomers into the circle and resist the temptation to exclude those who aren't just like you. That single mom, special-needs mom, or unmarried older woman is a sister, too!

Make Friends Outside Your Parish

A 2018 study by the Center for Applied Research in the Apostolate at Georgetown University found that only 20 percent of Catholic women attend church at least once a week.[7] This is a sad number, especially considering that we receive the real presence of Jesus Christ every time we go to Mass and receive the Eucharist. However, this means that there are ample opportunities to meet Catholic women outside of the parish.

If you meet Catholic friends outside of the parish and they do not attend Mass regularly, help point them back toward Mass and the Eucharist.

Invite your friends to attend a retreat or conference. Catholic women's events are proliferating around the country. Invite friends to attend with you, and introduce them to others from your community. Socialize with the people you have invited and help them to feel comfortable at the event, but balance this with taking time for your own prayer and reflection, and for connecting with others at the event. If you bond with someone at the event, make plans to keep in touch.

Look for Catholics in the community. We can be a pretty identifiable bunch. Be on the lookout for sacramental items such as crucifixes, Marian medals, scapulars, and rosary bracelets. Make a mental note when someone makes the Sign of the Cross while saying grace, or who comes to soccer practice with a smudged forehead on Ash Wednesday. Ask God to help you notice such people. Maybe that nice coworker who never eats meat on Fridays needs a spiritual friend.

Make yourself identifiable as a Catholic. I have a silly T-shirt that looks like a Starbucks logo, but it is actually an image of the Blessed Mother. The script around the periphery reads "I like her a latte." Every time I wear that T-shirt to Zumba, someone comments on it. It is a conversation opener. Live your faith boldly! Talk about Jesus as naturally as you would about your family or personal interests.

With even one Christ-centered relationship, and a shared desire to start or build a women's ministry, you are partway there. You do not need a lot of women to start a ministry, but you need a couple!

Form a Relationship with Your Pastor

In addition to Christ-centered relationships among the women, a women's ministry team needs to build a relationship with the pastor. Because the bishop entrusts the spiritual and pastoral care of the parish to the pastor,[8] a parish women's ministry and its direction should rightfully have the pastor's imprint and guidance.

Many pastors are happy to have vibrant women's ministries in their parishes. A healthy community of women growing in the faith will instigate growth throughout the parish, increase vocations, and support the pastor's duty "to take care of the catechesis of the Christian people so that the living faith of the faithful becomes manifest and active through doctrinal instruction and the experience of Christian life."[9]

Women can pray together, catechize each other, and enjoy fellowship, but if we want to remain close to the sacraments, especially the Eucharist, we can only grow so far without pastoral care. Keenly aware of the need for priests within her own ministry, St. Teresa of Calcutta wrote her bishop to request "all the spiritual help." She explained, "If we have Our Lord in the midst of us—with daily Mass and Holy Communion, I fear nothing for the Sisters nor myself—He will look after us. But without Him, I cannot be—I am helpless."[10] In fact, St. Teresa of Calcutta would not send her sisters anywhere without a priest.

The pastor usually knows the needs of his parish, and he has experience in guiding people through all the blessings and crosses of life. His pastoral care is a treasure and shepherding conduit to closer relationship with Christ. When Maggie suffered her miscarriage, our priest helped her unite her suffering to Jesus' Cross. Through the Sacrament of Anointing of the Sick, he provided an avenue for God's grace to heal Maggie and many other women who were not aware of their need for healing.

Breaking Down Barriers

I have a priest friend who exclaims, "Wow! Blessed am I among women!" whenever he meets with our women's ministry. That is how a women's ministry should make the priest feel: blessed, lifted in prayer, loved, respected, appreciated, and supported. Unfortunately, I know some priests who are leery—or even worse, *weary*—of women's ministry because they have felt more like referees to petty sniping than pastors. So, how can women's ministry foster a strong relationship, or even spiritual friendship, with their priest?

Get to know your priest and establish rapport. Seek his counsel and ask for his vision for the ministry. Your priest may have a clear direction for what he wants the women to do or learn. If so, listen, heed his instruction, and share your own ideas as well. Pray for him and remember important dates in his life, such as his birthday and ordination anniversary. Invite him to dinner with your family.

Invite, without pressure, your priest to women's ministry gatherings. The more you partner with the pastor, the better. Everyone benefits from more pastoral care. There may be times when women need privacy, but your priest could open or close your gatherings. As much as possible, accommodate *his* schedule. For example, if you want to incorporate Mass into your gatherings, plan to attend the parish's daily Mass and hold your women's gatherings immediately before or after the Mass.

Manage your own expectations carefully. Be mindful of the many responsibilities the priest has in the parish. If you want to talk about administrative aspects of the ministry, make an appointment. If you have a conflict or challenge in the women's ministry, come to him with a potential solution instead of just a problem. The priest's support of the ministry will increase as your relationship with him deepens.

---

momentum builders

TIPS FOR FOSTERING RELATIONSHIPS IN MINISTRY

This chapter explored developing spiritual friendships and fostering a relationship with your pastor, so let's set out to build these relationships.

Tip #1. Be on the lookout for spiritual friends. Characteristics of spiritual friends include the following:

○ They share beliefs in common so as to model and inspire virtue.
○ They listen and offer counsel that is consistent with the faith, speaking the truth with love.
○ They help carry each other's burdens in ways that unite our crosses toward Christ.
○ They celebrate God-given talents and gifts, without flattery or envy.
○ They seek harmony and unity. They ask for and grant forgiveness readily and accept correction that is given in love.
○ They are honest always, even when it would be easier to manipulate or placate.

Tip #2. Be active in the parish. Keep an eye out for opportunities to connect with women outside of the parish as well. Attract spiritual friends by living your faith boldly!

Tip #3. Seek pastoral care. Women's ministry needs pastoral care, especially to stay close to the sacraments. Forge a relationship with your pastor by getting to know him, seeking his input, and being mindful of his many responsibilities in the parish.

PONDER

Today's passage to ponder is from Sirach 6:5–10, 14–17:

> Pleasant speech multiplies friends,
> and gracious lips, friendly greetings.
> Let those who are friendly to you be many,
> but one in a thousand your confidant.
> When you gain friends, gain them through testing,

and do not be quick to trust them.
For there are friends when it suits them,
but they will not be around in time of trouble.
Another is a friend who turns into an enemy,
and tells of the quarrel to your disgrace.
Others are friends, table companions,
but they cannot be found in time of affliction. . . .
Faithful friends are a sturdy shelter;
whoever finds one finds a treasure.
Faithful friends are beyond price,
no amount can balance their worth.
Faithful friends are life-saving medicine;
those who fear God will find them.
Those who fear the Lord enjoy stable friendship,
for as they are, so will their neighbors be.

1. What does this passage from Sirach say about true friendship? How are you a good friend? How have your spiritual friends blessed you?
2. Are those you spend the most time with during the day spiritual friends? If so, how do they lead you toward living a life of virtue? If not, how can you be more intentional about investing in Christ-centered relationships?
3. Consider the role of the pastor in women's ministry. How do you seek guidance from your priest and include him in the women's ministry? How can you show your priest that you appreciate him?
4. Each parish ministry is a bit different, reflecting the needs and gifts of your particular group: How would you describe your parish's women's ministry now? What do you envision it becoming in the future?

Closing Prayer

Lord, thank you for the gift of faithful friends. Help us to be good friends to people we meet and to forge a strong relationship with our pastor. Give us eyes to be on the lookout for new friends in ministry and the temperaments to be dedicated, spiritual friends. Amen.

2

A Call within a Call:

DISCERNING A VOCATION TO WOMEN'S MINISTRY

> My God, give me courage now—this
> moment—to persevere in following
> Your call.
>
> —St. Teresa of Calcutta

SHARE

The first time a Catholic woman asked me what my vocation was, I had visions of the vocational wing of my high school, where students trained in technical fields such as automotive maintenance or electronics. I was confused, and I'm sure my contorted facial expression showed that I had no idea what *vocation* meant—at least not the way she used it. The woman explained that her vocation was to motherhood, which was why she was a stay-at-home mom at this point in her life.

I was perplexed. I was a busy parent trying to raise two young children, maintain a job, and put myself through law school. In addition, I had believed the lie that as women, we are valuable, good, or worthy of love, not because of our innate dignity, but because of what we do or accomplish. I felt compelled to prove myself to everyone through my productivity. Because of this, I was an over-volunteerer. I volunteered for the parent-teacher organization (PTO) and in my son's classroom; I led a Cub Scout den with thirteen unruly second graders; and despite zero athletic aptitude, I substituted as my son's soccer coach!

What was I thinking? I wish that someone had given me a big hug and said, "You are good enough even if you don't do it all, because God does not call us to do it all. And also, soccer clearly isn't your thing—you're making your son's soccer team lose!" I didn't want to think about my vocation; I wanted a *vacation* from managing the daily Tetris puzzle my life had become.

And yet, looking back, I realize that God was speaking to me through this woman's question and attempting to inspire me to examine my out-of-balance life. Her question prompted me to ask myself *why* I was doing this work in the first place: "What is your vocation? Why are you doing all this stuff?" I just did not know what vocation was, and more honestly, I was not willing to consider it.

Do you recognize yourself in this story? In your enthusiasm to make friends and build up a women's ministry, have you stopped to consider what is motivating you to act? Are you driven by the need to volunteer, or are you sensing a genuine call that springs from your vocation to grow closer to Christ? We each need to take a sacred pause . . . and consider the source of our motivation.

The Sacred Pause

I know what you're thinking: "Seriously, a pause? We're only on chapter 2, and we want to *do* the work of ministry!" Bear with me. Like Mary went to Elizabeth at the visitation, we "go in haste," but we cannot be *hasty*.

As you begin ministry work as a team, there is likely to be a lot of joy and enthusiasm. We are eager (if a bit apprehensive) to jump in and begin the work. In many Catholic communities, women have about two to three years to make friends and contribute positively to the community before passing the baton and moving on due to job changes, family circumstances, or other reasons. The urgency propels us.

While not all Catholic parishes are so transient, this sense of urgency can also be experienced by women who are prompted by the Spirit to act. A bishop once told me, "I learned a long time ago, don't get between a woman and her rosary beads." The same advice is equally sage for women beginning work in women's ministry—there is no stopping that initial joyful momentum.

So why do we need to take a sacred pause?

A sacred pause is like getting to the beach and putting on sunscreen before dashing into the surf. The preparation of slathering on SPF before diving into the water ensures that we will avoid debilitating sunburn, which in ministry equates to *burnout*. This preserves our ability to swim again, day after beautiful day, with peace and confidence that we are doing the work to which God calls us.

During this sacred pause we will explore two ideas. First, we will explore women's ministry as part of our Christian vocation. To do this, we will define *vocation* and look to Mary as a model of vocation. Second, we will explore how to discern our vocation in women's ministry with the life of St. Teresa of Calcutta as our role model and intercessor.

APPLY

DEFINING AND DISCERNING VOCATION

Vocation is a term frequently found in Catholic circles, but what does it mean? Our Christian vocation is a call to a closer relationship with Christ through marriage, religious life, or singleness (or, in the case of men, holy orders). However, vocation extends beyond our state in life (see *CCC* 898–900). The *Catechism of the Catholic Church* teaches that people "who with God's help have welcomed Christ's call and freely responded to it are urged on by love of Christ to proclaim the Good News everywhere in world" (*CCC* 3).

This definition shows us a few things.

First, our Christian vocation is premised on God's initial movement to call us to himself. God invites us to our vocation; we have to be open to the call and God's timing.

Second, God wants us to pursue our vocation. Indeed, God created each of us for this very purpose. Vocation is our free response to love Christ, and it is part of our continual conversion to grow closer to him.

Third, vocation is evangelistic. It involves becoming a missionary disciple—a person who professes faith in Christ, bears witness to it, and spreads the Good News (see *CCC* 1816).

Getting Started

What is behind your desire to get involved in women's ministry? We can be tempted to conflate volunteerism with our vocational work because both are often *pro bono* and for a greater good. Volunteerism, however, does not necessarily enhance our relationship with God. Anyone can volunteer, but as Christians we serve God and neighbor out of love. If we seek to build a women's ministry, we need to expand our thoughts and lexicon beyond *volunteerism* and *volunteer management*, and rephrase our discussion to women's ministry as part of our *vocation* and an endeavor in missionary discipleship.

Are we simply volunteering, or is our service part of our vocation? The question might sound harsh, but the answer is critical. Volunteerism is valuable in society, but if our service in ministry does not extend to our Christian vocation, our efforts will fall flat. For example, I used to volunteer with the PTO at my children's school by counting the soda-can tabs collected by the students. The school exchanged these tabs with soda manufacturers to raise funds for library books and computers. However, after a few months of this volunteer gig, I realized that I would rather do almost anything else than spend an hour flipping soda-can tabs. So I quit. Yes, I raised some money for the school, but I was not passionate about the PTO. Counting the soda-can tabs in no way felt like an expression of my love of God or that I was using my gifts and talents in heartfelt service. God intended something else for me.

As women, we express our love of God in many ways throughout our lives, and we can have more than one vocation, depending on our state in life and God's calling.[1] Single life, religious life, and married life are all vocations. Motherhood is a vocation that adds onto the vocation of married life. Single motherhood, too, is a vocation. A person's profession can also be a vocation.

In terms of how we serve God, we often have a primary vocation. My primary vocation is in married life, but I also have a vocation to motherhood, which complements my vocation to marriage, as my husband and I work to raise our children in the Catholic faith and love them the way Christ loves us—generously, sacrificially, and unconditionally.

A call to serve in a women's ministry is also a vocation. In fact, women's ministry is what St. Teresa of Calcutta described as "a vocation within a vocation," or "a call within a call." In women's ministry, we work to build faith-centered relationships that draw women closer to Christ and to each other, and build communities that instruct and assist other women to grow in the faith. The *General Directory for Catechesis* describes this as the "divine vocation" of the catechist.[2]

God created us as dynamic and multidimensional people, who have many avenues to love God and neighbor. The vocations within our overarching Christian vocation converge like a merge sign on the highway into one trajectory leading to Christ. Vocation can reside within all aspects of our lives, because, as Pope John Paul II wrote in *Familiaris Consortio*, love is the "fundamental and innate vocation of every human being" (sec. 11). St. Teresa of Calcutta states our vocation simply: "We have been create to love and be loved." So long as our work draws us closer to Christ, it can be part of our vocation.

Mary's Model of Vocation

As Catholics, we can look to the Blessed Mother as a model of all vocations. As we look at her life revealed in scripture, we see that she embodies five crucial qualities of living out a vocation: she was certain, joyful, steadfast, evangelistic, and sacrificial in difficult circumstances.

Certain. Consider Mary in Luke's gospel during the annunciation (see Luke 1:26–38). She began her maternal vocation when the angel Gabriel appeared to her and told her that she would give birth to Jesus.

At first, Mary questioned the angel's unexpected message: "How can this be, since I have no relations with a man?" (Lk 1:34). However, with her fiat, Mary gave her unwavering, certain assent to the angel's message. "Behold, I am the handmaid of the Lord. May it be done to me according to your word" (Lk 1:38). Mary was resolute. She attached no conditions to her yes, and she never looked back.

Joyful. In the visitation, we see that Mary's vocation is also joyful:

> During those days Mary set out and traveled to the hill country *in haste*, to a town of Judah, where she entered the house of Zechariah and greeted Elizabeth. When Elizabeth heard Mary's greeting, *the infant leaped* in her womb; and Elizabeth, filled with the Holy Spirit, *cried out in a loud voice* and said

"Most blessed are you among women, and blessed is
the fruit of your womb. And how does this happen
to me, that the mother of my Lord should come to
me? For at the moment the sound of your greeting
reached my ears, the infant *in my womb leaped for
joy.*" (Lk 1:39–44, emphasis added)

The excited exchange between the four people in this story—
Mary, Elizabeth, John the Baptist, and Jesus—brims with joy.
Mary went in a hurry; Elizabeth cried out; John leaped for joy.
Can you visualize their smiles? In the original Greek of Luke's
gospel, there were no punctuation marks. Nonetheless, modern
readers can hear the joy springing off the page. Mary shares pro-
found joy in her Magnificat, "My soul proclaims the greatness
of the Lord; my spirit rejoices in God my savior"(Lk 1:46–47).

Steadfast. Despite the early challenges of becoming the
Mother of God, Mary remained steadfast in her vocation. She
initially dedicated her life to nurturing Jesus in her womb and
giving birth to him in Bethlehem. Together with Joseph, she presented Jesus at the Temple to consecrate him to the Lord. Then
they fled to Egypt with him to protect him from King Herod.
Though Simeon warned Mary that her vocation would entail a
sword piercing her heart, she was undeterred. This steadfastness
is a mark of her vocation.

Once Jesus reached adulthood and began his public ministry,
Mary remained steadfast. For example, at the wedding at Cana,
when the party ran out of wine, Mary looked in faith to her Son,
and despite Jesus' seeming reticence—"Woman, how does your
concern affect me?" (Jn 2:4)—Mary was resolute in interceding
for the steward. When Jesus told the steward at the wedding to
fill six stone jars with water, this probably seemed strange. After
all, the steward did not need water; he needed wine. Nonetheless,
Mary advocated for Jesus like a loyal mama bear, "Do whatever
he tells you" (Jn 2:5).

Evangelistic. At Cana, Mary also demonstrated the evangelistic aspect of her vocation by sharing her belief in Jesus with the steward. In her direction "Do whatever he tells you," she communicated her belief in Jesus' ability to make water, something ordinary, into wine, something extraordinary. By her words and deeds she communicated that she believed in Jesus, and that perhaps the steward could share in her belief as well. Because Mary's work was vocational, she did not seek glory or adulation for prompting the miracle at Cana. To the contrary, Jesus himself was glorified through this miracle, and it enthused his disciples to believe in him (see John 2:11).

Sacrificial. Even when Mary's vocation brought suffering, she scarified out of love. Mary walked the Sorrowful Mysteries as closely as possible with her Son, praying through the night as he endured his agony in the garden of Gethsemane. She withstood her own agony as she watched Pontius Pilate wash his hands of Jesus' fate, leaving him to riotous crowds who chose Barabbas, a murderer, over her Son, a healer. She accompanied Jesus as he endured being crowned with thorns, mocked, beaten, stripped naked, and tortured with a cross whose weight challenged even Simon the Cyrenian. Mary loved Jesus through her presence at the Crucifixion, and she was obedient to him as he entrusted her to John the Beloved.

Mary's vocation compelled her to continue. In his *Pietá*, Michelangelo memorialized for the world that sorrowful but still unfaltering image of Mary holding her crucified Son's limp body. Certain and joyful at her initial call to her vocation, Mary was steadfast, evangelistic, and sacrificial in her vocation until her assumption into heaven (see *CCC* 966). This love is vocation.

Mary's work as Jesus' mother poignantly distinguishes volunteerism from vocational work. A volunteer faced with even a fraction of the challenge and personal sorrow that Mary endured would have quit long before the wedding at Cana. Mary remained with Jesus because this love was her vocation. Certain, joyful, steadfast, evangelistic, and sacrificial love is what we, too, are called to give in our vocation.

Work in women's ministry must be vocational to be sustainable. Volunteers in women's ministry quit when the initial joyful momentum and excitement is dampened by the friction of competing interests; the lure of other projects; or the discouragement of conflict, difficulty, or lack of recognition. Much like the fig tree that did not bear fruit, Jesus himself will cause a ministry group of volunteers to wither rapidly (see Mark 11:12–24).

Discerning a Vocation in Women's Ministry

With so many alluring ways to use our time and do good things in this world, we must discern how God is truly calling us to serve in our various vocations. We are finite people, with finite minutes in our days. We cannot do everything. Indeed, God does not call us to do everything. Discernment in the Christian life is a continuous spiritual conversation with God, ourselves, and spiritual friends or spiritual directors, through which we can make honest assessments of ourselves, make decisions, and act in accordance with God's promptings. God moves in our lives all the time, and his calling for us develops and changes through our phases in life, especially as we submit to God's will and grow in our relationship with him.

St. Ignatius of Loyola, the founder of the Society of Jesus (the Jesuits), wrote a series of Spiritual Exercises that can help us practice discernment. Ignatius described that during our lives we experience consolation and desolation. Consolation is characterized as "inflamed in love" of the Creator, with an abundance of faith, hope, and charity, and feelings of interior joy, closeness to God, and peace.[3]

In times of desolation we feel separated from God and lack faith, hope, and love. We may feel agitated, bored, or fearful. We may tend to be secretive about our struggles or behaviors. We can experience desolation because of our own sin or because God lets us experience challenges in our spirits. Ignatius cautions that in times of desolation, we should never make changes in our lives, but instead "remain firm and constant" in our decisions made in consolation.[4]

We can walk with God in both consolation and desolation, but discerning vocation occurs in consolation. In consolation, like the sheep who recognize the voice of their shepherd (see John 10:3), we are poised to recognize God's promptings and follow them with certainty.

─momentum builders─
ESSENTIAL QUALITIES FOR DISCERNMENT

As you discern how God is calling you to women's ministry, approach the process with the following Ignatian attitudes: (1) openness, (2) generosity, (3) courage, (4) interior freedom, (5) prayerful reflection, (6) setting right priorities, and (7) serving out of love and not our own ambitions.[5] Quiet yourself and ponder if you have these attitudes in discerning a call in women's ministry:

1. *Openness.* Discernment requires an open mind and heart and a willingness to set aside preconceived notions of what the ministry or your role will be. You may think that the ministry is going to be a weekly, one-hour Bible study, and that you will lead the study, but be open to the Holy Spirit. God may nudge you to something else. Are your mind and heart open?

2. *Generosity.* Generosity is the willingness to offer our desires and freedom to God without any conditions.[6] Generosity is living Mary's fiat, "May it be done to me according to your word" (Lk 1:38). Too often we say things such as "I will lead the women's social night, but only if Jeannie assists me." Strip away the conditions. Are you willing to serve generously?

3. *Courage.* Discernment requires courage to submit to what God calls us to—even if it is difficult or surprising. Are you courageous?

4. *Interior freedom.* With interior freedom, we let go of fear, pride, anxiety, other people's opinions of us, and anything else that keeps us from saying yes to God. Is there anything holding you back? If so, consider whether this impediment is God calling you elsewhere. Or maybe you need to let go of something.

5. *Prayerful reflection.* Discernment requires time to listen to God in prayer. Building this habit could entail setting aside time for a holy hour each week, reflecting on God's movement in your life at the end of each day, attending daily Mass, or gathering with other ministry leaders to talk about how you all feel called to serve. How do you carve out time for reflection?

6. *Setting right priorities.* If serving God is our life's goal, everything else must support that end. What is the primary way in which you serve God? This could be as a wife, mother, or caregiver of elderly parents; maybe it is as a working professional or in a call to religious life or missions. Serving in women's ministry is good so long as it enhances our primary vocation. We have to be careful that we don't get so wrapped up in activities that we feed scraps to our primary vocation. Are there opportunities—even *good* opportunities—that you need to say no to in order to better serve God in your vocation?

7. *Serving out of love.* Ignatius wrote that the "eye of our intention ought to be single . . . to praise God our Lord and save my soul. Anything whatsoever I elect ought to be chose as an end toward that aim."[7] We serve a women's ministry out of love.

Sometimes, however, women use women's ministry service to further their own interests: "I don't have a job right now, but maintaining the ministry's budget will help keep my resume active." Or, "My kids are in school now, and I need something to occupy my time." This logic turns what should be vocational into something self-serving.

A better way to think about serving is: "I love helping women grow closer to Christ. As a teacher, I am equipped to teach Bible study, and I have the desire and time to do so." The end in this discourse is putting your gifts and time into God's service. While enhancing your resume may turn out to be an added benefit, your primary motivation remains, "Am I serving out of love?"

These essential attitudes prepare us spiritually to enter a process of discernment. If you are not ready, talk to your pastor or a spiritual friend about what is holding you back.

――――――――――――――――――

As you discern whether women's ministry is part of your vocation, and how to serve in a women's ministry, try to identify the primary question—the issue that is at the core of your discernment process. For example:

- Should I start a parish women's ministry?
- Shall I organize a pilgrimage for my women's ministry?

Once you have identified the primary (or "threshold") question, let any noise surrounding this question fall away. Other ancillary questions—which room you will meet in; whether anyone will participate in the ministry—are distractions at this point. Focus on the threshold question of whether it is part of your vocation to serve in the ministry. Once you have identified what you are discerning, consider the practicalities:

- Would saying yes to this decision enhance or distract from my primary vocation? Do I have the time, competence, and commitment to say yes? Do I *want* to serve in this capacity?
- What guidance does my spouse, spiritual friend, or trusted priest who knows about my strengths and weaknesses have to offer me about this decision? Who should I ask to help me explore the decision?
- Do I have clarity in the decision? Yes or no can both be holy decisions, because the goal of discernment is to align your will with God's. If your decision is a holy no, it means that God is calling you elsewhere for now.
- Don't be afraid of making a wrong decision when choosing between two good things. After you have made a decision, move forward prayerfully. Expect that if God wants you to serve in a different capacity, he'll let you know.

If you make a decision to serve in women's ministry, God will give you confirmation that you have made the right decision. Discernment yields joyfulness of spirit and the peace and certainty that you are serving God.

St. Teresa of Calcutta, Intercessor for Women's Ministry

Look to St. Teresa of Calcutta as an intercessor as you discern your vocation in women's ministry. St. Teresa of Calcutta's vocation, first as a Sister of Loreto, and later as the founder of the Missionaries of Charity, offers a clear example of discerning God's call and living out our vocation.

When St. Teresa of Calcutta was in her teens, she engaged in a period of discernment about her vocation to become a Sister of Loreto. While she discerned her vocation, she described that she was happy at home with her family but, "[W]hen I was eighteen, I decided to leave my home and become a nun. . . . I have never doubted for a second that I've done the right thing; it was the will of God. It was His choice."[8] She expressed her vocation to serve as a Loreto Sister in a letter to the Mother Superior: "I want to join your Society so that one day I may become a missionary sister, and work for Jesus who died for us all."[9] Mother Teresa's response of love was to spread the Good News as a missionary disciple. She told the Mother Superior, "I don't have any special conditions, I only want to be in the missions, and for everything else I surrender myself completely to the good God's disposal."[10]

St. Teresa was a Loreto Sister for more than a decade until God spoke to her directly and called her to serve the poorest of the poor. Over several years, as Teresa discerned God's call to found the Missionaries of Charity, she consulted with her spiritual director. She was emphatic that God wanted her to remain a religious sister but perceived the call to serve the poorest of the poor as a "call within a call."[11] Teresa's spiritual director told her to draft proposed rules (founding documents) for the new religious community. In this way, he helped her pause to "test the spirits" to see whether they were from God (1 Jn 4:1).

In the rules of the Missionaries of Charity, Mother Teresa described her vocation "to satiate the thirst of Jesus Christ on the Cross for Love and Souls." She continued, "Jesus is God: therefore, His love, His thirst is infinite. Our aim is to quench this infinite thirst of a God-made man." Mother Teresa shared that when Jesus said, "I thirst," on the Cross, "He spoke of His thirst—not for water—but for love, for sacrifice."[12] This infinite work to quench the thirst of Jesus for souls is the vocation of the Missionaries of Charity, and as a call within a call, it enhanced Teresa's vocation to religious life.

Teresa knew that only vocation, and not volunteerism, would make the work of the Missionaries of Charity fruitful. She said, "If our work were just to wash feet and give medicines to the sick, the center would have closed a long time ago. The most important thing in our centers is the opportunity we are offering to reach souls."[13]

What Next?

We know that vocational work out of love of Christ will not always be easy. God never promises that our work will be easy; he asks us to trust as he leads. I asked a gathering of women's ministry leaders why they stay involved even when the work gets tough. These ladies stay involved for the same reasons they were excited about starting the work in the first place. Dollia said, "I keep at it because it's my vocation within a vocation. I am closer to God with service to Catholic women and redemptive suffering." Another friend said she stays involved because she feels "called to serve . . . it is not for us to see the fruits of our labor." Denise shared, "Leading/assisting Catholic women's ministry is beneficial for my personal faith journey. [I am] always strengthened by others who God places in my path!" Aimee wrote, "I feel called. I enjoy it. I love growing with others and helping others grow."

These ladies made me smile because they collectively articulated that women's ministry is part of their vocation. In their unique ways, they voiced that they are obedient to the call to serve and that God strengthens their faith through women's ministry and increases their joy. I have to agree with these ladies. Through participating in women's ministry, God has blessed me with much growth in faith, deepened my love for him, and inspired me to use what gifts God has given me to spread the Good News.

—momentum builders—
TIPS FOR DISCERNING
GOD'S CALL

Tip #1. Distinguish between vocation and volunteerism. Working in women's ministry is not volunteerism. It is a vocation, a "call within a call" that we pursue because we love Christ zealously and want to help other women grow in their relationship with Jesus.

Tip #2. Look to God for guidance and strength. When you are working within your vocation, you will feel certainty that you are doing the work to which God calls you, joyful in the work, steadfast in your efforts, evangelistic in sharing the Gospel with others, and sacrificial in continuing even when your work may be difficult.

Tip #3. Don't overlook the practical realities. Take time to ask God how he is calling you to serve in women's ministry. Perhaps he is asking you to take on a limited role or to participate for a short time. Allow God to guide you as you work out the practicalities of how serving in women's ministry fits within your Christian vocation.

The faithful are called to hand down the faith "from generation to generation, by professing the faith, by living it in fraternal sharing, and by celebrating it in liturgy and prayer" (*CCC* Prologue 3). This is the vocational work of women's ministry. Though the personality or charisms of women's ministry might change in different communities, the love of Christ compels women to press on. St. Teresa of Calcutta wrote that the work of a Missionary of Charity "is not strewn with roses, in fact more with thorns; but with it all, it is a life full of happiness and joy when she thinks that she is doing the same work which Jesus was doing when He was on earth, that she is fulfilling Jesus' commandment: 'Go and teach all nations!'"[14]

Through taking a sacred pause to consider your vocation and discerning how God is calling you, I hope that you will keep up the joyful momentum, serve selflessly and sacrificially, and even reprioritize other interests if needed. If you have explored your vocation in women's ministry and know that God is calling you to this work, then you are ready to jump into the surf!

PONDER

Today's passage to ponder is Mary's Magnificat, which is found in Luke 1:46–56.

> And Mary said:
>
> "My soul proclaims the greatness of the Lord;
> my spirit rejoices in God my savior.
> For he has looked upon his handmaid's lowliness;
> behold, from now on will all ages call me blessed.
> The Mighty One has done great things for me,
> and holy is his name.
> His mercy is from age to age
> to those who fear him.
> He has shown might with his arm,
> dispersed the arrogant of mind and heart.
> He has thrown down the rulers from their thrones
> but lifted up the lowly.
> The hungry he has filled with good things;
> the rich he has sent away empty.
> He has helped Israel his servant,
> remembering his mercy,
> according to his promise to our fathers,
> to Abraham and to his descendants forever."

> Mary remained with [Elizabeth] about three months
> and then returned to her home.

1. Read the passage slowly and meditate on the text. In which words do you particularly hear Mary's joy? Where do you find joy like hers in your life? Is this joy a fruit of your vocation?
2. Describe a time when you felt joyful momentum about a new endeavor. Did the initial excitement last? Why or why not?
3. Have you ever allowed yourself to become overcommitted? Why did this happen? What did you do about it? Did you make the decisions that led to your overcommitment during a time or consolation or desolation?
4. If you feel "a call within a call" to women's ministry, how does this call fit within other vocations in your life? Are there aspects of your work that do not fit within your vocation? If so, are there things you need to stop doing to make room to serve within your vocation? Talk with a spiritual friend about this.

Closing Prayer

St. Teresa of Calcutta, you accepted the call to satiate Jesus' infinite thirst for love and souls and became a carrier of his love to the poorest of the poor. Pray that in discerning our vocation, we may receive clarity, peace, zeal, and joy. May we long to satiate the burning thirst of Jesus by loving him ardently, sharing in his sufferings joyfully, and serving him wholeheartedly in our vocation. Amen.

3

United in Hope:

CULTIVATING CHRISTIAN HOSPITALITY

Live simply so that all may simply
live.
—St. Elizabeth Ann Seton

SHARE

We had been living for several years in West Point, New York, when Greg returned from a deployment and the army gave him new orders to Fort Bliss, Texas, which adjoins the city of El Paso. In preparation for the move, I flew to El Paso to house hunt and find schools for our children. This was the first time I had been without my children in months, and the solitude felt foreign and unsettling. I was so accustomed to corralling kids that I did not know what to do in the calm of my airplane window seat. This was also the first chance I'd had to process the upcoming move and consider the impact on our family.

Unfortunately, I let pessimism take hold. I looked forward to having my family reunited but resented having to find new schools, new friends, a new dentist, new doctors, a new church—really, new everything! I was sad that this would be the fourth school in five years for our oldest son, and I was upset about

losing my job and the progress that I had made in my professional endeavors. Moving to west Texas meant starting over. I
mulled over these circumstances on the westward flight and
watched as cities and towns below gradually faded into desolate
orange desert.

I was like a child with a skinned knee. Have you ever tried
to persuade a child who has just fallen off her bike and skinned
her knees that she really will learn to ride a bike? Telling her that
things will get better is not too helpful because she cannot see
beyond the scrapes. It seems hopeless. I needed someone who
would offer to comfort the pain, encourage me to try again,
and run alongside me until I regained confidence and my hope
was restored. I was in dire need of some authentic Catholic
hospitality.

It wasn't difficult to see the reason for my desolation. I was
spiritually fatigued from the deployment year and too depleted
to expend energy on new endeavors. Some military spouses
thrive when their service member is gone. I do not; I barely hold
on. Our family starts extended separations with well-intended
diversions such as making construction-paper link chains that
the kids can shorten each day to count down toward their father's
return. After a few months, however, we neglect crafty rituals
and just mark time. I slip into sloppy habits such as skipping my
gym workout and binging on pizza. I retreat from friendships
that offer loving support because I do not want to admit to anyone that the grief that comes with Greg's extended absences is
almost insurmountable for me.

On the descent into El Paso we flew over tumbleweeds and
abandoned buildings. This harsh terrain mirrored my mood,
and I thought, "What have we done? Why are we moving here?"
Our family sat figuratively perched on the top of a roller coaster
tipping beyond the precipice and moving as inertia dictated. I
could put on my big-girl pants and throw up my hands with
hopeful anticipation of the opportunity ahead, or I could close

myself off and resentfully curse the experience. Either way, we were moving to El Paso.

And you know what I did? As a thirty-three-year-old woman, I refused to put on my big-girl pants. To be theologically precise, I lacked the virtue of hope. Hope is the theological virtue by which we desire the kingdom of heaven and place our trust in Christ's promises rather than our own strengths. Hope keeps us from discouragement, sustains us when we feel abandoned, and opens our hearts in expectation of God's will. "Buoyed up by hope, he is preserved from selfishness and led to the happiness that flows from charity" (*CCC* 1818). In our Christian walk, hope is desiring and expecting union with God. Pope Benedict XVI wrote that when we have hope, we become "ministers of hope" and are prepared to serve others (*Spe Salvi* 34).

APPLY
HOPE IN GOD'S HOSPITALITY

In any situation, we must strive to rejoice in hope—real hope. But how often do we misuse the word *hope*? We say things such as "Hopefully it won't rain" or "Let's hope for the best." We relegate the virtue of hope to a filler word. Or worse, we say "hope" when what we really mean is "I desire selfishly." Conflating the virtue of hope with selfish desire is what I did during the move to El Paso. I barely considered God's will at all and saw our move as an obstacle to what I desired for the sake of my own comfort and ambitions. I failed to realize that God had something more in store.

As it turns out, from the myopic aperture of my bad attitude and miniscule airplane window, I could not see *physically* the beauty of El Paso's desert mountains or the greenness of the Rio Grande Valley. I lacked the hope to see *spiritually* God's hospitality extended in the beautiful memories we would form, the friendships that awaited us at the Catholic school that my children would grow to love, or the women's ministry that would embrace me.

The tragedy of faltering in hope is that our focus shifts away from God, and we fail to see his hospitality in our lives. This can happen in big things such as a cross-country move. It also happens in little things, such as standing in the slowest checkout line ever. Rather than persevering in the minute inconvenience of waiting in line, we tap our toes, scan the aisles for a shorter queue, and sigh loudly when the clerk turns on the price-check light. And so, when the clerk finally gets to us and thanks us for our patience, we can avoid eye contact and quip tersely at the clerk's best efforts—or we can receive the attempted hospitality. When we choose to be uncharitable and refuse hospitality even in small things, it is a failing of hope.

Getting Started

In his encyclical on hope, Pope Benedict XVI quotes St. Augustine, who said that we lack hope because our hearts are full of vinegar, which God wants to purge so that there is room for God to move within us. According to Augustine, God wants to fill our hearts with the honey of hope and stretch our hearts to increase in hope (*Spe Salvi* 33).

When we lack hope, we can fall into the sin of despair, which is ceasing to hope for salvation from God, or the sin of presumption, the idea that we do not need God but can do everything on our own (see *CCC* 2091, 2092). When we experience any type of suffering or challenge in life, we must pray for an increase in hope in order to see God's movement all around us.

Practicing hospitality increases hope. The word for hospitality in the New Testament is *philoxenia*, which means to love (*phyllo*) strangers (*xenia*). Through our baptism, we have "clothed [ourselves] with Christ" (Gal 3:27) and become living stones to build the Church. We are "called to be subject to others, to serve them" (*CCC* 1269). We are directed to "be hospitable to one another without complaining" (1 Pt 4:9). Paul reminds the Romans that they are one body in Christ and must "love one another with mutual affection" (Rom 12:10). He directs them to "Rejoice in hope, endure in affliction, persevere in prayer. Contribute to the needs of the holy ones, exercise hospitality [*philoxenia*]" (Rom 12:12–13). Jesus' words on hospitality are clear: "As I have loved you, so also should love one another" (Jn 13:34). In extending hospitality, we build up the Church and bear witness to Christ.

We are called to extend hospitality to others—whether stranger or friend—freely and without expectation of returned favor. Ideally, though, hospitality becomes not just a one-sided action but an integrated dance in which the host serves another person and the recipient is inspired to accept the hospitality and, in turn, serve someone else. Reciprocation is a fruit of hospitality. In this way, hospitality becomes mutual and evangelistic. However, an introit to this hospitality dance is the premise that the recipient has sufficient hope to recognize and accept the host's hospitality in the first place.

In women's ministry, we must meet people just where they are. Sometimes people come to us with abundant hope, a great love of God, and eagerness to serve others. If so, great! Recruit that person to help the ministry serve with hospitality. Other times, people come to a women's ministry with a lot of challenges to their hope. They may be weary, burdened, or suffering. Through sharing hospitality we can bolster other people's hope, help them mature and find meaning in their suffering, and encourage renewal in their trust in God.

Hospitality in Women's Ministry

Hospitality is one of the most important aspects of a women's ministry. Through our hospitality we welcome women over the threshold and into the fold of the ministry. As we incorporate hospitality throughout our gatherings, we affirm their worth in the eyes of God and inspire them to return week after week. Finally, their reception of our hospitality increases hope and inspires them to share that hospitality with others, both inside and outside the group. So, hospitality is a vital way to share the faith.

While hospitality can be expressed in many ways, some of the most critical in women's ministry is in the invitation, the welcome, and the gathering itself.

Hospitality in the invitation. At our new parish in El Paso, the women's ministry extended generous hospitality to me. Shortly after the school year started, I toted a book by a Catholic author to the local coffee shop and settled into a well-worn leather chair for some quiet reading. A Latina with long, dark hair sat down next to me, saw my book, and asked, "Are you Catholic?" I told her that I was.

"Me, too!" In her excitement, her accent made it a bit hard to follow what she was saying. "We have an amazing women's ministry group. You should come! We pray the Rosary, then we have faith study. And we have Mass!" Then she sealed the deal. "And there's free childcare." Free childcare? Sign me up!

Hospitality in the welcome. My new friend told me that the group was meeting the following day, adding apologetically that she was unable to make it that day. Brushing aside her apologies, I accepted her friendly invitation with renewed hope (and curiosity). As she left, she expressed her hope that we would see each other again.

Since food is my love language and I wanted to put my best food forward, I arrived armed with a breakfast casserole. When I stepped into the parish's religious-education building, I was completely blown away by the warmth of this community. The women were playing lively music, and a table in the entryway was beautifully set with a picture of our Blessed Mother and a small vase of flowers. Two ladies at the table welcomed everyone. They wore name tags, so I was able to call them by their names, and they called me by my name. I felt welcome and at home.

A lady helped me deliver my casserole to the buffet and asked me about myself. I shared that I had three children and had just moved to the area. With that, my new friend led me around the room and introduced me: "This is Elizabeth. She just moved here. She has three children . . ." The introductions took the pressure off me, a newcomer, and allowed me to inch my way into circles of established friends. The hard part for a newcomer is sometimes just walking through the door. This simple hospitality reduced any reticence.

Hospitality in the gathering. The hospitality continued in the way the women organized their Rosary group; they consistently lowered any barrier to participation and prayed in a way that encouraged everyone to join at her comfort level. If you did not know how to pray the Rosary, or if you did not have a rosary, no worries! Someone circulated a basket with instruction booklets and beaded rosaries crafted by ladies in the group, with a note inviting women to borrow or keep a rosary. The leader invited women to share their prayer intentions, and as she wrote them on a whiteboard, she reminded everyone that intentions should remain confidential.

After the Rosary, we enjoyed the potluck breakfast then split into smaller groups for a faith study, where there was something for everyone. Each small group studied a different Catholic book or video series. There was a scripture study, a book about deepening prayer, one on missionary discipleship, and one about the vocation of motherhood. Young or more "seasoned," as the group called it; married or single; introspective or outward-oriented;

new to the faith or thoroughly catechized; and everything in between—there was a study for everyone.

At the end of the gathering, the hospitality continued with an invitation to Mass. Beginning the morning with the Rosary, breakfast, fellowship, and study, and ending with Mass, was the perfect way to spend a Friday morning and exactly the hospitality that I needed as I embraced El Paso. This format assured that we were able to observe the one-hour fast before receiving Communion. The gathering didn't involve flashy entertainment but rather a consistent dance of invitation and acceptance that always pointed toward Christ.

These women increased my hope. Regaining hope in our move to El Paso took time, and I cried a lot of tears as the "vinegar" drained out of my heart. The transition from West Point to El Paso taught me that we have to throw up our hands in surrender and tip over the precipice of a new experience in expectation that God will refine us through any suffering and put people in our way who will put on Christ for us. With renewed hope, I realized that people all around me were extending hospitality—I just needed to accept it.

St. Elizabeth Ann Seton, a Model of Hopeful Hospitality

In his encyclical on hope, Pope Benedict XVI explains that purification leading to hope is something very personal; it is an encounter between ourselves and God. This interaction must be guided by the prayers of the Church, the saints, and the liturgy (*Spe Salvi* 34). As ministry leaders, we can look to St. Elizabeth Ann Seton as a role model and intercessor to help us cultivate the virtue of hope and practice hospitality.

Born in 1773, Elizabeth, the first American-born saint, lived through the American Revolution in New York City. Elizabeth's mother died when Elizabeth was a child, and she was raised by her father, a prominent physician, and stepmother. In 1794, Elizabeth married a tradesman, William Seton. The couple settled into married life in a Wall Street row house and were blessed with five children in eight years. A devout Anglican and naturally inclined to hospitality, Elizabeth cared for widowed mothers and provided them with essential household items.

In 1803, Elizabeth's comfortable life was uprooted by a storm of hardships reminiscent of Job. William's business collapsed, forcing him toward bankruptcy. Her father died of typhus contracted while caring for immigrants quarantined in New York Harbor. Additionally, William was suffering the late stages of tuberculosis.

William and Elizabeth traveled with their oldest child to Livorno, Italy, to the home of Filippo and Mary Filicchi. Filippo became her husband's mentor in the shipping trade. William intended to seek business counsel from Filippo, and the science of the day taught that the mild climate would aid William's tuberculosis. By the time the fragile family arrived in Livorno, William was visibly ill and the Setons were placed in the harbor's quarantine prison—*lazaretto*, in Italian, after St. Lazarus.

Conditions in the lazaretto were so severe that Elizabeth and her daughter jumped rope together to keep warm as her husband lay "on the old bricks without a fire, shivering and groaning, lifting his dim and sorrowful eyes with a fixed gaze in my face while his tears ran on his pillow without one word."[1] There was little rest for the Setons, as a group of shipwrecked, quarreling sailors occupied a neighboring cell.

Anyone's hope would have been challenged at the lazaretto, but with heroic virtue Elizabeth persevered. She wrote to a friend that there was "no hope of (William's) recovery in the view of MORTAL HOPES" [emphasis in original], yet she also expressed "how gracious is the Lord who strengthens my poor soul."[2] Elizabeth felt close to God during this suffering and found that God gave her peace. She wrote to a friend, "Sometimes I feel so assured that the guardian Angel is immediately present that I look from my book and can hardly be persuaded that I was not touched."[3]

Elizabeth received what hospitality could be offered with gratitude. The warden was kind and provided the Setons with mattresses, shared food from his family's storehouse, and reduced the quarantine period, knowing that William was dying (he later attended the funeral as a final corporal work of mercy). The Filicchis extended hospitality by visiting the lazaretto gate to wave at Elizabeth, reassuring her that she was not alone, sending food, and even delivering a bed to replace William's mattress. William died shortly after leaving the lazaretto.

Suddenly Elizabeth was transformed from a benefactress of poor widows to a thirty-year-old insolvent widow and mother of five. In such adversity, Elizabeth could have allowed vinegar to fill her heart, refused the hospitality offered to her, or behaved like the shipwrecked sailors. Instead she maintained hope. Even when her eyes were swollen from crying, she wrote, "I must close them and lift up my heart."[4]

After William's death, the Filicchis extended the hospitality of their Catholic faith to bring spiritual comfort to an Anglican widow. They introduced Elizabeth to the Mass, where she came to believe in the real presence of Jesus in the Eucharist. She also came to know the Blessed Mother and realized, "[R]eally I had a Mother which you know my foolish heart so often lamented to have lost in early days."[5]

Elizabeth's story gives a powerful example of hope and how God works through others to buoy our hope. Though the warden and the Filicchis could not take away Elizabeth's suffering or grief, they are keen examples of exercising hospitality and pointing Elizabeth toward Christ.

Practicing hospitality is one of the most important ways that a women's ministry can serve the needs of others, and it inspires women to participate in the community. A women's ministry gathering is made up of ladies from all walks of life, experiences in the Church, and backgrounds. A hospitable women's ministry does what the warden and the Filicchis did for Elizabeth. The community must meet each person exactly where she is in life and serve her needs. If she is rejoicing, the community should rejoice with her. If she is suffering, the community should accompany her to help her journey in hope and find meaning in the suffering.

Elizabeth initially needed basic items such as a fire for warmth, food, a bed to care for her husband, and gestures of encouragement. As her circumstances changed and her husband died, Elizabeth needed the comfort of the Catholic faith. Her community met those needs with compassion, which means to suffer (*passion*) with (*com*) another person, and helped guide her toward her eventual conversion to Catholicism.

When I first arrived in El Paso, my community extended hospitality and met me exactly where I was. I needed an invitation to join the women's ministry, and an astute stranger in a coffee shop invited me. I needed friends, and women greeted me and made introductions. I needed to reconnect to my faith after the deployment year of barely holding on, and the ministry provided opportunities for Bible and faith study. Finally, and most importantly, I needed to meet God in the sacraments, and the ministry pointed me to Mass every week. While my suffering was nothing compared to what Elizabeth Seton endured, I did not have her hope to sustain me. When we lack hope, when we are in a place of desolation, we cannot see beyond ourselves.

Sometimes in women's ministry, people come to us without hope. We may not perceive their suffering as being too difficult, but we must be humble and avoid judgment. Serve these people and help them mature in hope. As Paul points out, "We have gifts that differ according to the grace given to us" (Rom 12:6). In serving each other with hospitality, we must be careful to realize that each person is uniquely situated in her journey of conversion; none of us is perfected yet. Augustine describes that when our hearts are emptied from vinegar, God will strengthen our desire for him. God wants to increase our hope (*Spe Salvi* 33). To bring an increase in the virtue of hope should be a goal of our hospitality in ministry.

We may never fully realize how our hospitality affects or inspires others. After returning to New York from Italy, Elizabeth Seton converted to Catholicism and founded a religious order, the Sisters of Charity of St. Joseph, and she is credited with establishing Catholic schools in the United States. The warden and the Filicchis did not know that their hospitality would help lead Elizabeth to convert to the Catholic faith. They served her out of love of God and neighbor.

Because hospitality is about loving others as Christ loves us, we must have hope to know that even if our hospitality is not immediately met with a response, it does not mean that we have neglected to do what God wants. It could mean that the person is not open to being served because they lack hope, or that the Holy Spirit is working on the person in ways that we do not perceive. Try not to be discouraged. Paul reminded the Galatians, "Let us not grow tired of doing good, for in due time we shall reap our harvest, if we do not give up" (Gal 6:9). As sure as Elizabeth heard the boorish behavior of the shipwrecked sailors in the lazaretto, they heard her caring for her husband in the next cell. History did not record what happened to these sailors, but Elizabeth's hope and hospitality provided an example to them and to us.

Cultivating Hope, Practicing Hospitality

Increasing in hope takes God's grace and our own diligence in prayer and perseverance. As we lean on God's grace to help us remain hopeful in little things, we will get better at retaining hope in bigger challenges. Here are some practical ways to build hope and encourage others to be hopeful:

- *Pray daily for an increase in hope.* On the first three Hail Marys of the Rosary, we pray for an increase of the theological virtues of faith, hope, and charity. Pray the Rosary and be especially mindful of that prayer for hope.
- *Recognize when you start to lack hope.* When you find yourself spinning in pessimism or negativity, recognize this as a failing in the virtue of hope. If you are in a bad place, and there is vinegar in your heart, purge it through prayer and the sacraments. If we experience desolation, it can be hard to find the words to talk to God. In these times, rely on the prayers of the Church and the liturgy to make room for the Holy Spirit to move.
- *Invite or permit someone to walk with you.* If there is something challenging your hope, name it and face it with good friends. When Elizabeth Ann Seton suffered the death of her husband and her hope was challenged, she wrote letters to her friends and relied on the Filicchis to help her through. Accept hospitality.
- *Look for the Beatitudes in your life.* St. Benedict wrote, "Incline the ear of your heart" to God. To increase in hope, ask the Holy Spirit to help you notice the blessings in your current situation. Each Beatitude starts with a blessing— "Blessed are the . . . ," "Blessed are the poor in spirit . . ." (Mt 5:3)—and each ends with a promise—"for theirs is the kingdom of heaven" (Mt 5:3, 10). Look for the present blessing in your life, and anticipate God's blessing through it. Searching for blessings helps us to "rejoice in hope" (Rom 12:12).
- *Practice gratitude.* When you see God's blessings, write them down. Review your list of blessings daily, or weekly, and thank God for these gifts. Thank the people who bless you.

- *Strive to see good intentions in others' actions.* Pray that God will help you see others' actions with the best of intentions. Consider who may be trying to extend hospitality to you or increase your hope. Are you open to receiving it?
- *Pray for perseverance and surround yourself with encouragers.* Several years ago, I was gravely ill. My beautiful friend Kelly told me, "Don't waste this suffering." She encouraged me to offer the suffering up in prayer and accept it. Those were hard words to hear because I did not want to suffer! But I was so weak that I could not stand long enough to retrieve food from the refrigerator. As the weeks went on, Kelly's words stuck with me, and I tried to offer my suffering for others whenever I felt discouraged. Kelly stuck with me, too. She generously went with me to doctor's appointments and took notes for me so that I could refer to them later to understand what was happening. Her encouragement carried me. Encouragers help us press on in hope.
- *Seek counsel.* If you are in an unhealthy emotional place or suffering from depression, anxiety, or another psychological challenge, seek spiritual counsel or mental health counseling. Psychological health is equally important as physical health. God wants our happiness.

Hospitality in women's ministry can be light and social to draw people in and pique their interest to return. It can also be a more deliberate endeavor to put the corporal and spiritual works into action, such as the good Samaritan who reached out to the wounded stranger, treated his injuries, carried him to shelter, and provided for the care he needed. Be sensitive to the spiritual wounds of those you encounter, and treat them with the same tender, loving care in the name of Jesus.

How? Consider the follow suggestions to practice hospitality in a ministry.

- *Make the parish your primary place of meeting.* Why? First, we are eucharistic people, and we need to gather around the "source and summit of the Christian life" (*CCC* 1324). Second, a women's ministry that meets at the parish is accessible to everyone in the community. If the gathering meets primarily in a person's home, new people may feel like interlopers, or they may not know of the gathering at all. Third, the quiet, protected space within a parish lends itself to private conversation. If the group primarily gathers at a café or other public place, women may be less inclined to share. Can you meet outside the parish? Absolutely! But if you are building a women's ministry for the parish, spend time in the parish.

- *Have a hospitality team to accompany newcomers to the group.* This team would assist new people with introductions, gather and share their contact information, connect them through email distribution lists or social media, and help them find their niche in the ministry. At a gathering, the hospitality team could incorporate ice breakers or games as fun ways for ladies to help each other get acquainted. (Don't forget the door prizes!)

- *Create an inviting meeting space.* As the daughter of a US Marine, I grew up attending religious-education classes in Quonset huts and can attest that good catechesis can happen in rusty, corrugated aluminum buildings. However, if you can, consider creating a little ambiance in your meeting space. Set the tables with flowers, candles, tablecloths, and a picture of the Blessed Mother or an icon of the patron saint of your group. Add a crucifix into a centerpiece. If children are welcome, have a space where they can play, color, or watch movies.

- *Break bread together.* Like I said before, food is my love language. Sharing a potluck meal is a simple way to encourage women to serve one another and take a little ownership in the ministry. A meal facilitates conversation, and lending an ear to another's experience is a grace of hospitality.

- *Foster opportunities for women to serve each other.* "As each one has received a gift, use it to serve one another as good stewards of God's varied grace" (1 Pt 4:10). An easy way to do this is to give women particular roles in the ministry or tasks to coordinate: leading faith study, coordinating meal sign-ups, planning a retreat, setting up childcare, organizing ladies' night out or other social gatherings, updating social media and sending emails, facilitating outreach or service projects. These roles can change depending on the charisms of the group, and we will discuss this in detail in chapter 4, "Gifted to Serve."

- *Be a cheerful giver.* "Be hospitable to one another without complaining" (1 Pt 4:9). If you get stuck in a rut or find yourself complaining about the work that you *have* to do in ministry, go to God in prayer and ask him to renew your spirit, refine your vocation, and help you pare down the to-do list so that you can serve with joy. Talk to a partner in ministry about whether you have slipped your vocation into volunteerism. St. Teresa of Calcutta taught that "if you do your work with joy, you can bring many souls to God. Joy is prayer, a sign of our generosity, evident in our eyes, our faces, our actions."[6]

- *Seek to understand.* Sometimes in life, and ministry, a person may refuse to accept our best efforts at hospitality. If you experience resistance, take counsel from St. Paul: "Endure in affliction, persevere in prayer" (Rom 12:12). This will preserve your hope. Also, take heart—there might be a reason that the person is rejecting your hospitality. A friend in our women's ministry was going through chemotherapy. Though the ministry tried to bring her meals during her treatments, she declined. She explained that she was afraid of getting sick, so she did not want to eat food that was not prepared the way her body was accustomed to. We asked if her family had a favorite restaurant and if we could order meals for them instead. She agreed, so instead of cooking dinners, our ministry blessed her with restaurant gift cards. It was an easy way to put on Christ for her while respecting her wishes.

- *Reciprocate hospitality.* As we experience Christlike hospitality in our community, our hope increases—so we can share it with others! If you receive an invitation to the women's ministry gathering, reciprocate the hospitality by inviting someone else. Ask the Holy Spirit to put this person in your path.
- *Let someone serve you.* By accepting hospitality, you are allowing someone to serve you with Christ's love, and you are increasing that person's joy. An example of this is when a mom brings her baby to a women's ministry gathering. So often, if the baby fusses, women scurry to rock the baby, comfort the baby, or even change a diaper. Moms do a great service in letting other women help. In my current women's ministry group, one of the more "seasoned" ladies is a widow and a retired pediatric nurse. Her children have long since left the nest, and her grandchildren live in another state. She loves serving young moms by helping with their crying babies, and the young moms do a great service by accepting her help.
- *Express gratitude.* When someone shares hospitality, thank them. Send a kind email, a thank-you note, or a small gift to those who are serving you. A small act of encouragement may inspire someone to keep serving.

momentum builders
TIPS FOR INSPIRING HOPE THROUGH HOSPITALITY

Tip #1. Ask God to infuse your spirit with hope. When we are hopeful, we desire God and are more likely to seek opportunities to serve others. If you lack hope, pray for an increase in this virtue, let friends in ministry walk with you, and lean on the grace of the sacraments.

Tip #2. Practice intentional, unconditional acceptance and welcome. In offering hospitality, we serve others out of the love of Christ. This means accepting people as they are and embracing them, spiritual wounds and all.

Tip #3. Look for ways to be more welcoming in every aspect of ministry. Hospitality is one of the most important parts of a ministry because it brings people to their first gathering and keeps them coming back. Be sure to extend hospitality in all aspects of the ministry—from the initial invitation, to the gathering, and even to renewing the invitation.

PONDER

Today's passage to ponder is Luke 10:30–37, the parable of the good Samaritan. In this parable, a "scholar of the law" tests Jesus with a seemingly innocuous question: "Who is my neighbor?"

Jesus replied, "A man fell victim to robbers as he went down from Jerusalem to Jericho. They stripped and beat him and went off leaving him half-dead. A priest happened to be going down that road, but when he saw him, he passed by on the opposite side. Likewise a Levite came to the place, and when he saw him, he passed by on the opposite side. But a Samaritan traveler who came upon him was moved with compassion at the sight. He approached the victim, poured oil and wine over his wounds and bandaged them. Then he lifted him up on his own animal, took him to an inn and cared for him. The next day he took out two silver coins and gave them to the innkeeper with the instruction, 'Take care of him. If you spend more than what I have given you, I shall repay you on my way back.' Which of these three, in your opinion, was neighbor to the robbers' victim?" He answered, "The one who treated him with mercy." Jesus said to him, "Go and do likewise."

1. This parable is likely very familiar to you. Did something stand out to you this time? What characteristics of hospitality do you see in this parable?
2. Consider a time when your hope was challenged. What was the challenge, and how did you overcome this situation? How have you matured in hope since then? Who helped you, and what did that person do? Consider sending that person a note of thanks.
3. Reflecting on women's ministry, how has someone served you with hospitality? How did this affect your hope? Did you reciprocate the hospitality to this person, or toward someone else?
4. Think of a time when you felt welcomed into a new community. What did others do to make you feel welcome? How does your community welcome newcomers? Make a list of at least five ways that you can help new people feel welcome.

5. If you have an active women's ministry, think of your group's primary meeting. From the beginning of the gathering to the end, list all the ways that your group practices hospitality. What are at least three ways that you can improve? If you are starting a women's ministry, consider how you will incorporate hospitality into your new group.

Closing Prayer

Lord, with St. Elizabeth Ann Seton as role model of heroic hope, help us increase in the virtue of hope. Guide us to recognize and appreciate hospitality from friends in ministry. As ministry leaders, help us see and respond to opportunities to put on Christ for others. Amen.

4

Gifted to Serve:

OFFERING OUR CHARISMS

> Every pious desire, every good
> thought, every charitable work
> inspired by the love of Jesus, con-
> tributes to the perfection of the
> whole body of the faithful. A person
> who does nothing more than lov-
> ingly pray to God for his brethren,
> participates in the great works of
> saving souls.
>
> —Blessed Anne
> Catherine Emmerich

SHARE

My friend Victoria is a naturally caring, introverted, and faithful soul. When Victoria attends women's ministry gatherings, she brings a shoebox filled with her collection of CD recordings of presentations by Catholic speakers that she has amassed over the years. She places the box on a table at each gathering with a sign-out sheet and invites women to borrow CDs as often as they would like. Victoria's lending library offers a quiet, steady witness of faith and a needed catechetical resource beyond our weekly gatherings.

I have personally benefited from Victoria's service. Like many moms who attend our gatherings, I do a lot of children chauffeuring and commuting between work and home. The CDs help reorient the narrative filling my brain from whatever is on the radio to something that teaches me about the faith or helps me pray.

No one in the women's ministry (other than the Holy Spirit) asked Victoria to start a lending library, but once she began sharing this gift, it became an integral part of the ministry—a resource that the group did not know we needed. In offering her CD lending library, Victoria shares several charisms, or spiritual gifts. Wisdom and evangelism come to mind. Because she has the charism of wisdom, she perceived the group's need for catechesis. Her gift of evangelism, paired with her natural introversion, helps her spread the Gospel message by loaning CDs.

Charisms, or "spiritual gifts," are different from our skill sets, which are things such as our professional training, education, learned behaviors, life experiences, personalities, physical abilities, and leadership styles. We pray for the graces of charisms and the discernment to know how the Holy Spirit calls us to use them. While we can train and practice our skill sets, the Holy Spirit determines how much of a gift to entrust to each person. Both charisms and skill sets are important in ministry; we employ our skill sets to put our charisms into service. Though we cannot increase spiritual gifts on our own volition, we can—and should—ask God to give (and increase) spiritual gifts to us to help us serve the Body of Christ. A little later, we will talk about the different charisms that the Holy Spirit bestows on individuals.

APPLY
UNDERSTANDING THE CHARISMS

When we encourage women to serve in a ministry, we must be careful to invite them to use not just their skills but their charisms as well. If we assign people to ministry roles based on skill sets alone, we slip into conflating service with utility and risk missing the Holy Spirit's prompting. The call to serve in ministry is to share our spiritual gifts, not merely to use our skills.

It may be difficult at times to distinguish a spiritual gift from a skill. One way to think about this difference is that skills make the spiritual gift tangible. Teaching, for example, is a spiritual gift. We train our skills to serve with this spiritual gift by learning the subject matter and relevant teaching methods. Skill sets are essential to serving in ministry, but they support—as opposed to eclipse—the spiritual gift. The Church recognizes that the measure of a spiritual gift is not skill but "charity, the true measure of all charisms" (*CCC* 800).

Getting Started

Spiritual gifts, or charisms, "whether extraordinary or simple and humble," are "graces of the Holy Spirit which directly or indirectly benefit the Church, ordered as they are to her building up, to the good of men, and to the needs of the world" (*CCC* 799). Each woman is uniquely gifted with charisms, and we are to accept these gifts, which are diverse and complementary, with gratitude (see *CCC* 800, 801). As Paul wrote, "For as in one body we have many parts, and all the parts do not have the same function, so we, though many, are one body in Christ and individually parts of one another. Since we have gifts that differ according to the grace given to us, let us exercise them" (Rom 12:4–6). Romans 12:6–8, 1 Corinthians 12:4–31, and Ephesians

4:11–13 are the main passages from the New Testament that teach us about the types of spiritual gifts:

- *Prophesy.* People with this gift have an intuitive ability to recognize God's work and truth and proclaim it forthrightly to others (see Romans 12:6; Ephesians 4:11; 1 Corinthians 12:10).
- *Ministry or helps.* This gift prompts people to serve in genuine love for the edification of the community. It can mean lending a hand or taking action to spread the Gospel (see Romans 12:7; 1 Corinthians 12:28).
- *Teaching.* Teaching is the gift of understanding the faith and imparting it to others. This spiritual gift may be made manifest formally through offering catechesis and joining in missionary discipleship, or through everyday interactions such as reading to a child (see 1 Corinthians 12:28; Ephesians 4:11).
- *Exhortation.* This is the gift of bringing out the best in others through encouragement and instruction. The Holy Father, for example, recently issued *Gaudete et Exsultate*, an apostolic exhortation on the call to holiness in today's world to encourage the faithful to grow in virtue (see Romans 12:8).
- *Leadership.* Leadership—or as Paul writes, "if one is over others, with diligence" (Rom 12:8)—is a forward-looking gift that gathers people and points people toward God. Leaders hold up a flashlight to help others see where and how God is calling us as individuals and as a community.
- *Mercy with cheerfulness.* Someone with this gift possesses the ability to have compassion for and alleviate the suffering of another. Some might call this the gift of compassion (see Romans 12:8).
- *Wisdom.* Whereas the gift of faith is a simple knowledge of the articles of Christian belief, wisdom goes on to a certain

divine penetration of the truths themselves (see 1 Corinthians 12:8; James 1:5).

- *Knowledge.* Knowledge involves the understanding of Christian doctrine (see 1 Corinthians 12:8).
- *Faith.* Faith is believing in God by grace and the help of the Holy Spirit, trusting in God, and cleaving to the truths he has revealed (see *CCC* 154). Faith is also one of the three theological virtues (see 1 Corinthians 12:9).
- *Administration.* The gift of administration is often visible in someone who organizes people, processes, or things, or coordinates members of a group (see 1 Corinthians 12:28).
- *Healing.* Healing, whether in body or spirit, "make(s) manifest the power of the grace of the risen Lord" (*CCC* 1508). We serve with this gift by caring for those who suffer through offering the corporal and spiritual works of mercy and accompanying them with intercessory prayer (see 1 Corinthians 12:9).
- *Mighty deeds or miracles.* A miracle is something beyond the order of created nature or natural law.[1] This spiritual gift could be performing a miracle through the grace of God, but it could also be the grace of receiving a miracle, such as a healing deemed to be medically impossible, so that the healed person may bear witness to God's grace (see 1 Corinthians 12:10, 28).
- *Discernment of spirits.* This is the ability to consider a course of action, or to read or hear a teaching, and know whether it is from God (see 1 Corinthians 12:10).
- *Tongues.* This gift allows someone to speak to God in a language with which they are not familiar (or to interpret another person's speech for the benefit of others) (see 1 Corinthians 12:10).
- *Apostleship.* This term comes from the Greek *apostelo*, meaning "I send out." As Catholics, we most often associate this with the gift Jesus gave to the apostles and their successors,

the bishops, commissioning them, "Go, therefore, and make disciples" (Mt 28:19), and handing over to them "the authority to teach in their own place" (*Dei Verbum* 2:7, 8). And yet the gift of apostleship can also be manifested in a broader sense by the laity, to anyone who "goes out" to share the faith to those who do not know Jesus (*Apostolicam Actuositatem* 1). For example, Mary Magdalene, the "Apostle to the Apostles," is an example of a woman who had this spiritual gift. She was the first person to whom Jesus entrusted the joyful news of his resurrection.[2]

- *Evangelism.* To evangelize means to spread the Good News. In modern day, evangelism is "missionary discipleship," where, through the prompting of the Holy Spirit, we share the Gospel message and accompany others as we grow in faith of Jesus (see Ephesians 4:11).

- *Pastoring.* This gift involves leadership of a congregation or faith community. Pastors are called to carry out the functions of teaching, sanctify, and governing, with the cooperation of other presbyters or deacons and with the assistance of lay members of the Christian faithful[3] (see Ephesians 4:11).

As you probably noticed, charisms and the ways we serve with our gifts overlap like a Venn diagram. It may be difficult to parse out whether someone is serving with the gift of ministry, compassion, or both. But knowing which gifts a person uses with precision misses the point. The point is that our spiritual gifts work in concert to build the Church.

Since everyone has unique spiritual gifts and skills, it is not surprising that this diversity makes each women's ministry unique. Even if women use the same spiritual gifts, our service will be different because our skills and personalities bring another layer. For example, think of how people with extroverted or introverted personalities might share the spiritual gift of evangelism. An extrovert might be naturally inclined to strike up conversations about her relationship with Jesus with strangers on elevators. An introvert may evangelize by sharing her faith with a friend or in a small-group discussion. Both methods of evangelism are equally important to propagating the faith.

Complementary Gifts in Ministry

Our uniqueness is something to celebrate. St. Thérèse of Lisieux had a spirituality of serving God in her "little way," with simple acts. One time, she wondered why God does not give the same graces to everyone. Jesus revealed to Thérèse that each person, like every flower that God creates, "has a beauty of its own." She came to understand that "the splendor of the rose and the lily's whiteness do not deprive the violet of its scent nor make less ravishing the daisy's charm." Together, we form a vibrant and fragrant bouquet, and God delights in each one of us: "Just as the sun shines equally on the cedar and the little flower, so the Divine Sun shines equally on everyone, great and small."[4]

Pope John Paul II also praised the unique ways that God gifts women, and he thanked us for serving with our gifts. In his *Letter to Women*, John Paul II thanks us as mothers, wives, daughters, sisters, workers outside the home, consecrated women, "and in fact all women."[5]

Sadly, we sometimes fall into the temptation of yielding to self-doubt or insecurity about our giftedness. We are tempted to compete with one another or to compare our spiritual gifts. This can lead to pride, jealousy, or envy. Sometimes we even criticize ourselves for not being gifted enough, or for not doing enough, as if the number of tasks we can accomplish are measures of our worth or value. This can lead to a lack of charity toward ourselves or ingratitude for failing to appreciate all that we are. We end up wasting time trying to feel good enough to serve the Church, instead of simply serving. We honor God by being exactly who he created us to be. God has given us exactly the graces that we need to serve now—we are already ready!

Competition and comparison are thieves of joy and surefire ways to sink a friendship or paralyze a ministry. Don't give in to these temptations. Instead, consider Thérèse's words:

> It pleases him to create great saints, who may be compared with the lilies or the rose; but he has also created little ones, who must be content to be daisies or violets, nestling at his feet to delight his eyes when he should choose to look at them. The happier they are to be as he wills, the more perfect they are.[6]

A friend in ministry distills the substance of Thérèse's truth in her own way. She says that in women's ministry, "We don't compete; we complete." Celebrate the gifts of others because diverse gifts yield diverse rewards. Let's celebrate, shall we?

Let me give you an example of how this can work even on a very large scale, such as a global ministry. For two years I was president of the women's ministry for the Archdiocese for the Military Services, USA. The ministry gathers US military–affiliated women from around the globe and builds a spiritual community to grow in faith and service. The ministry holds spiritual retreats annually in geographic regions around the world. Every other year we hold a faith-formation forum, which gathers women from across the globe to a weekend event in United States.

The night I agreed to take this role, I asked the archbishop what my focus should be for the two-year term. "Formation," he said. I met with the new team the next morning and brought to the table my spiritual gifts, including leadership, teaching, and administration. I also brought my skill sets, including my educational background in theology, my professional training as a lawyer, my deep desire to include everyone, and my analytical thinking style.

Over the next two years we prayerfully set our formation goals, and worked to achieve them. One goal was to increase participation at retreats and other faith-formation events through improved communication. While the reach of the ministry was global, we hugged the community closer by building a digital community through creating a blog authored by about twenty women and increasing our presence in social media platforms. Participation more than doubled in two years, and our blog readership and social media engagement grew steadily. These metrics indicated that women enjoyed the ministry and word was spreading.

While I relied on my spiritual gifts and strengths to serve the ministry, I also depended on the other women to bring their spiritual gifts and skills to the team. Exhortation is not one of my greatest spiritual gifts. I had to work to be an encourager and motivator for a team of women, especially when the members were diffusely located in eight different states as well as Germany and Korea.

Thankfully, several women on the team were spiritually gifted with exhortation. I relied on my friends in ministry—Dollia, Michelle, Erin, and Marcia—and the exhortation and other charisms that they brought to the team. These women were steadfast in seeing the gifts and service of others, and encouraging them with their words, notes, and prayers. They also encouraged me to be more mindful of the need to pray for the gift of exhortation and to practice encouraging the women.

During the two-year term we had enough funding to meet only once in person for a weekend; all of our other meetings involved a dozen women joining in a conference call that spanned nearly all the time zones of the world. Given that this weekend retreat was our only time to talk face-to-face, I was determined to cram tons of action items into our meeting agenda. When I shared the draft agenda with my friend Marcia, she stopped me. With her gifts of wisdom and exhortation, and her incredibly relational personality, Marcia perceived something I did not. She called me, and in her endearing British accent said, "*Dahling*, don't do so much business. You need to get to know these women. Take time to get to know each other. Okay, mate?" She was right.

With her counsel, I cut down the agenda and made space for a retreat and for friendships to form. We created time for each woman to spend with a prayer sister from the team. One woman who had a background in teaching led us in a team-building workshop. We visited a Catholic shrine, had a social dinner together, and even enjoyed a white elephant gift exchange with wine and snacks. The in-person gathering accomplished the essential work that we needed to do and helped us get to know the personalities and personal stories behind the voices on the conference calls. That meeting created the momentum for the rest of our term. Had it not been for Marcia's wisdom and exhortation, I would have plowed forward, oblivious to the need to slow down.

Each woman on the leadership team contributed to the ministry's movement and growth in her unique way. Erin put her gifts of teaching, exhortation, and evangelism into practice with her skill set in curriculum development. Kim brought her gifts of administration and ministry, and her professional background in nonprofit management. Michelle offered her gifts of exhortation and ministry, and her skills in event planning. She cheered and encouraged us throughout the two years and planned a retreat for military women in our Pacific region.

The team served diligently, and we formed lasting friendships. Our two years of service culminated at our faith-formation forum in Washington, DC, where I passed the leadership baton to Michelle. Upon taking the reins, Michelle, in turn, had dinner with our archbishop and asked what her focus should be. Again, he instructed, "Formation." The purpose of the ministry would not change; however, the ways that God has uniquely gifted us was apparent in *how* the ministry worked toward faith formation. As our archbishop remarked to us in conversation, "Each leader brings her own richness" to the ministry.

Where my approach was prayerful and methodical, Michelle's was prayerful and expansive. One day in conversation, Michelle let herself be vulnerable with me. She said, "Elizabeth, I can't do what you do!" She explained that she did not know how to do the technical skills such as creating a website and scrutinizing a budget. I responded, "Michelle, you don't have to do what I did! I can't do what you do! You just have to find the right people." She offered her spiritual gifts, and with her knack for networking she found a woman to serve as the webmaster. She asked me to stay on as her advisor and invited new women to serve in ways that the ministry had not done before. For example, under her leadership the ministry launched a prayer program for mothers.

Mary and Martha's Complementary Gifts

One of the great examples of women with complementary gifts is found in the Gospel story of Jesus' close friends Mary and Martha of Bethany, the sisters of Lazarus. Their unique gifts are apparent in how they interacted with Jesus in the Gospel of Luke:

> [Jesus] entered a village where a woman whose name was Martha welcomed him. She had a sister named Mary [who] sat beside the Lord at his feet listening to him speak. Martha, burdened with much serving, came to him and said, "Lord, do you not care that my sister has left me by myself to do the serving? Tell her to help me." The Lord said to her in reply, "Martha, Martha, you are anxious and worried about many things. There is need of only one thing. Mary has chosen the better part and it will not be taken from her." (Lk 10:38–42)

A cursory glance at this passage may make it seem as if Mary is the more spiritual or faithful woman. Some use this passage to create a dichotomy between the two sisters. Crafty signs on Etsy and Pinterest read "Give me Martha's hands but Mary's heart." But to this I say no! The point of the story is not to compare and contrast two of Jesus' friends. The world needs all of Martha and all of Mary, and God is refining each of them. More importantly, God loves all of Mary and all of Martha.

In this solitary snapshot of their story, Mary chose the better because she did not give in to anxiety or become overburdened. Mary teaches us how to rest with Jesus even when there is bustle all around us. Mary models how to prioritize. The dishes can wait; time with Jesus cannot. She reminds us that having everything in order is not a prerequisite to approaching Jesus because he wants to meet us in the ordinary muck of household chores. She gives an example of resisting the temptation to control situations and, instead, resting in the present moment.

Mary may have possessed the spiritual gift of discernment of spirits; she modeled resting in Jesus rather than telling us how to rest. Perhaps her personality was deeply intuitive or shy. Her life experiences may have taught her not to stress over circumstances that cannot be changed—such as having Jesus and his followers show up for dinner. If she were a part of a modern women's ministry, Mary might naturally gravitate to serving as a sacristan, mentoring younger women, leading a Rosary group, or teaching Bible study. A modern-day Mary is the woman who spends time with Jesus at eucharistic adoration. Someone with the gifts of teaching, to provide verbal catechesis, might complement Mary in ministry. Do you know a woman like Mary?

Meanwhile, Martha is just as essential to the work of ministry. She teaches us what to do with our burdens and anxiety so that we can get to a point in our spiritual lives where we, like Mary, can rest with Jesus. Martha shows us to take our anxiety directly to Jesus when she says, "Lord, do you not care that my sister has left me by myself to do the serving? Tell her to help me" (Lk 10:40). Can you hear Martha's plea to Jesus as a prayer resonating in your own life? It might go something like, "God, I am overwhelmed. I have a million things to do. I am worried and stressed out! Will you please help me?" How many times have you prayed this sort of prayer? We are all a bit like Martha.

Jesus tells us that Mary chose "the better," not that Martha chose the bad. Did you catch that? Martha, too, chose the good. The alternative to Martha's plea to Jesus is choosing not to talk with God. Martha never stops talking with Jesus, and through this she teaches us to persevere in prayer.

What are Martha's spiritual gifts? The way she serves in a hands-on manner suggests the gift of ministry or administration. Her personality may be practical, efficient, or even bossy, yet she wears her heart on her sleeve. Martha is a doer. In a modern women's ministry, Martha may be drawn to the corporal works of mercy, planning an event, and taking charge of the logistics. As a complement to her ministry, Martha may need encouragement from someone with the spiritual gift of exhortation to remind her to avoid trying to fix or do everything on her own. Do you know a person like Martha?

While Mary and Martha are uniquely gifted, they also possess some of the same gifts, such as evangelism—sharing the message of Jesus. Mary evangelizes her belief in Jesus through her actions. It was Mary who "took a liter of costly perfumed oil made from genuine aromatic nard and anointed the feet of Jesus and dried them with her hair" (Jn 12:3), demonstrating her devotion to all present.

Meanwhile, Martha made a verbal declaration of faith. When Jesus arrived at their home to raise Lazarus from the dead, Jesus challenged Martha, saying, "I am the resurrection and the life, whoever believes in me, even if he dies, will live, and everyone who lives and believes in me will never die. Do you believe this?" Martha responded directly, "Yes, Lord. I have come to believe that you are the Messiah, the Son of God, the one who is coming into the world" (Jn 11:25–27). Her statement is one of the first professions of faith in the Gospel. Perhaps another one of Martha's spiritual gifts is prophesy—the ability to recognize and speak God's truth. In their uniqueness, Jesus loved Mary and Martha and wrapped them into the fold of his ministry. Their diversely gifted complementarity grew one Church.

Spiritual Gifts and Conversation Starter

Look for natural opportunities to talk about spiritual gifts. We have to help women discover their spiritual gifts and use them in ways that complement each other. We can come to know our spiritual gifts through prayer, observation, and conversation. One method to help women explore their spiritual gifts and how to share them is to facilitate a conversation using the Spiritual Gifts and Service Conversation Starter below.

Spiritual Gifts and Service Conversation Starter	
What do you enjoy doing?	What do you want to learn?
What excites you?	What are you tired of doing?

At the start of the discussion, have each person take a few minutes to jot down their thoughts about each of these four boxes, then compare notes after reading together the following:

What do you enjoy doing? When we consider what we enjoy doing, we often find that what we enjoy is not the act of doing but the spiritual gift behind it. For example, my beautiful friend Carolyn has a devotion to St. Bernadette and Our Lady of Lourdes. Pilgrims seek healing graces when they visit Lourdes, and many miracles have been attributed to having contact with water that bubbles from the grotto. Carolyn enjoys sharing Lourdes water with anyone who is suffering. Her prompting to share Lourdes water is the spiritual gift of healing. She does not physically heal anyone, because we know that healing comes from God, but by sharing Lourdes water, she is a conduit for healing people's bodies and spirits.

What do you want to learn? When we consider what we want to learn, we get a sense of where the Holy Spirit is prompting us to use our spiritual gifts; it's a holy curiosity. For example, my friend Laura teaches nonverbal autistic students. One year, as her school's Christmas concert approached, she was told that her students would not perform with the chorus because they could not sing like the other students. Undeterred, Laura learned of a keyboard app that her students could use on a tablet to play melodies of carols that they knew but could not communicate through song. Using tablets, Laura's students performed Christmas carols at the concert. Through learning about the app and teaching it to her students, Laura shared the spiritual gift of helps.

What excites you? Excitement reveals opportunities in ministry. For example, Christine, my friend in ministry, was always excited about travel and making pilgrimages to holy sites. She researched Catholic shrines in our area and led her small group on a pilgrimage to the National Shrine of St. Elizabeth Ann Seton in Emmitsburg, Maryland. The group enjoyed the pilgrimage so much that they began scheduling pilgrimages several times a year. Within two years, they visited sites in the DC area, including the National Shrine of St. John Paul II; the Basilica of the National Shrine of the Immaculate Conception; St. Matthew's Cathedral; and St. Patrick's Church, which is where President Kennedy prayed before his inauguration. Beyond the initial group, Christine saw an opportunity to invite women's ministries from other parishes to join the pilgrimages, and our outings grew in numbers and enriched in friendships. Christine's spiritual gifts of teaching, administration, and evangelism became tangible through harnessing excitement about pilgrimages into planning and leading pilgrimages.

What are you tired of doing? Asking what we are tired of doing reveals an important difference between spiritual gifts and skill sets. We do not get tired of our spiritual gifts, but we may grow tired of sharing them in a certain way. For example, my friend Sarah went through a time in women's ministry when she was the secretary of the group. She updated email lists and social media, and she took minutes at planning meetings. For a while, she liked the role because it was administrative, behind the scenes, and forward-thinking. Eventually, however, she found herself avoiding what she once enjoyed. She procrastinated on writing the meeting minutes and became irritated when people gave constructive feedback. She wanted to teach rather than complete her secretary duties. As a servant in ministry, she had burned out, and she spoke up. Sarah knew that continuing in the role would breed resentment, and that in stepping aside, another woman would bring her spiritual gifts and enthusiasm to the ministry. Her partners in ministry helped her shift the secretary role to a woman who wanted to serve. Sarah trained the new secretary and then stepped back into participating in gatherings with a cheerful spirit.

Sarah was not tired of her gift of administration; she was tired of taking minutes. If we are tired of something, the Holy

Spirit may be prompting us to make a change—to use a new skill, learn a new skill, or serve somewhere else.

Asking this question can also provide opportunities for the ministry to grow or improve in ways that ministry leaders might not otherwise have considered. I once led a retreat in Missouri in which a woman shared that she was "tired of drama" in the ministry. Her bold statement opened the door for the ministry to consider some unhealthy gossip and jealousy in the group and to refocus on serving with their spiritual gifts instead of sniping at what they perceived as one another's shortcomings. They had fallen into the temptation of focusing on Martha's anxiety at the expense of seeing her faithfulness.

—momentum builders—
TIPS FOR DISCOVERING AND INTEGRATING SPIRITUAL GIFTS IN MINISTRY

Depending on how familiar you and your team are with your spiritual gifts, you might decide to spend some time exploring and mapping out how those gifts are represented and used in your ministry. Here are some tips to assist you in this process.

Tip #1. Host a charisms retreat. Use the sample below to help women explore and dialogue about their charisms. Work with a team to incorporate hospitality and extend a broad invitation. This retreat might include the following elements:

- *Worship.* Begin with Mass. (30–45 minutes)
- *Fellowship.* Share a potluck breakfast. (30 minutes)

- *Catechesis.* Invite one of the women in the group, your priest, or a Catholic speaker to share a talk on serving with our charisms. (45 minutes)
- *Personal reflection.* Give each participant personal reflection time to complete the Spiritual Gifts and Service Conversation Starter. Let the women wander into the church or outside to have time to reflect. Play soft music to encourage a spirit of quiet. (30–45 minutes)
- *Sharing.* Invite the women to share their insights in small groups of two or three participants. Ask each group to name the charisms that they notice in each participant. Write the names of the participants and their charisms on a whiteboard. The facilitator should guide the session by encouraging the ladies to offer their charisms, then ask ministry leaders to continue discussion of how to put the charisms into action. (1 hour)
- *Prayer.* Close the mini-retreat with saying a Rosary or other communal prayer. (20 minutes)

Tip #2. Consider the current fit of gifts and responsibilities. Once you have a better understanding of the spiritual gifts represented in your community, as a team consider the best ways to integrate these gifts into your ministry. Are there new opportunities and needs you might not have considered in the past, that these gifts could fill?

Tip #3. Chart out current responsibilities and adjust as needed. If you have not already done so, take time to chart out roles and duty descriptions for your current leadership team. Consider how these responsibilities are being carried out in light of this new information about the gifts, skills, and interests of your community. (A list of suggested job descriptions is available as a download at joyfulmomentum.org or avemariapress.com.[7])

═══════════════════════════════

Whether you feel that God has graced you with the gifts of a large tiger lily or a tiny lily of the valley, have confidence that

God has particularly gifted you to serve, and he will equip you to build the Church. As St. Thérèse wrote, "Our Lord's love shines out just as much through the little soul who yields completely to His grace as it does through the greatest."[8]

PONDER

Today's passages to ponder focus on three New Testament women, each of whom played a significant role in the Early Church: Lydia (Acts 16:13–15) and Lois and Eunice (2 Tim 1:3–5). In the first passage, Luke writes:

> On the sabbath we went outside the city gate along the river where we thought there would be a place of prayer. We sat and spoke with the women who had gathered there. One of them, a woman named Lydia, a dealer in purple cloth, from the city of Thyatira, a worshiper of God, listened, and the Lord opened her heart to pay attention to what Paul was saying. After she and her household had been baptized, she offered us an invitation, "If you consider me a believer in the Lord, come and stay at my home," and she prevailed on us.

In the second passage, Paul writes to his beloved spiritual son Timothy about the spiritual legacy Timothy received from his grandmother and mother.

> I am grateful to God, whom I worship with a clear conscience as my ancestors did, as I remember you constantly in my prayers, night and day. I yearn to see you again, recalling your tears, so that I may be filled with joy, as I recall your sincere faith that first lived in your grandmother Lois and in your mother Eunice and that I am confident lives also in you.

1. Though scripture does not tell us a great deal about these women, what do you think were some of their charisms? We do not always need to know a lot about someone to discern a charism, because charisms stand out. What are some charisms that stand out among women in your ministry, especially among the women you do not know very well?

2. Complete the Spiritual Gifts and Service Conversation Starter. Share your answers with a friend or in your ministry group. Did anything surprise you? Based on this, how are you—or how are you not—using your spiritual gifts in the way that God is calling you? (You may need to continue this conversation with a spiritual director.)

3. Share about a time when you felt certain that you were serving with your unique spiritual gifts. Did anyone encourage you in sharing those spiritual gifts? How?

4. Consider the position descriptions, which you downloaded from the website. Are there necessary tasks that your ministry's leadership team needs to include in your job descriptions? Based on the interests and needs of your community, should other ministry roles be created? If so, invite women in the community to consider taking on these new roles.

5. Think of someone you know who is currently using their spiritual gifts to build the Church. Acknowledge that person this week. Name what you have observed as their gifts in conversation, by sending a note, an encouraging text, or an email. You will be sharing the gift of exhortation, which is always needed in women's ministry!

Closing Prayer

Lord, your servant St. Thérèse reminds us that Jesus does not ask for glorious deeds. He asks only for self-surrender and for gratitude. Help us to submit in surrender to your will and recognize and embrace the charisms that you bestow on us. Remind us to celebrate and encourage our sisters in Christ to use their gifts and skills to build the Church. Keep us ever grateful of the gifts you have given us. Shield us from insecurity or pride in our service, and unite us in perfect charity. We ask for St. Thérèse to intercede as we discern our gifts to serve in ministry. Amen.

5

Go to the Well:

"INREACH" AND OUTREACH

> I hope our Lord will teach me to do
> His will. I see Him thirsty at the well
> and tired. I wish to slake His thirst,
> according to His Will and in the
> manner He wills.
>
> —St. Katharine Drexel

SHARE

When my daughter entered first grade, I made the transition from being a stay-at-home mom to going back to work full-time. I had spent two years at home and loved the time with my children, but I was ready and excited to get back into the legal profession. Upon returning to the workforce, the irrational fear that my brain had turned to mush during years of dabbing finger paints and molding playdough, observing kindergarten ballet classes, and teaching "Hooked on Phonics" lessons was laid to rest. My brain had not atrophied. Our family adjusted to the new schedule, and while we had to be careful to safeguard family time and continue our ritual after-dinner strolls and bedtime reading, we made it work.

I initially planned to spend a lunch hour once a week with my women's ministry Bible study but soon gave up on that as thoughts of lunchtime Bible study were quickly replaced with efforts to learn the law firm's business processes, the substantive law in a new practice area, and the temperaments of unfamiliar judges. The lunch hour afforded me an occasional trip to the office coffee maker but not much more. I simply could not hew out time to stay connected with my women's ministry during the business day.

Unfortunately for me, our parish's women's ministry met only during the workday. The ministry was a dedicated community of mostly stay-at-home moms who were military wives, retirees, or older moms who no longer had children in the nest. These women were wonderful, but women who worked outside the home did not have the opportunity to get to know them during the daytime gatherings.

Our parish included a lot of women—including many women on active military duty—who worked during the day. Like me, they did not have time on their lunch breaks to attend Bible study with regularity. A common chorus during discussions in our daytime group was, "We should reach out to the active-duty women." People would chime in with yeps and affirmative nods but then unceremoniously move on to the next topic. The expressed desire to reach out to professional women did not align with our actions.

Within a few months of starting work, I began to crave the connectivity that I had enjoyed during my stay-at-home mom years. I missed studying scripture with other women, attending daily Mass, and keeping up with prayer requests and the normal developments in my friends' lives. Maintaining contact with my ministry group via phone calls from my car on the way to court, or exchanging text messages, could not replace in-person interactions.

Fortunately the daytime gathering decided to reach out to working women and added an evening book club to the ministry's offerings. The intent was twofold. First, it would create an

opportunity for women who worked during the day to participate, especially active-duty service members. Second, the book
club would provide a diverse offering to women looking for an
alternative to the weekly Bible study.

My friend Erin led the book club and selected fiction and
nonfiction titles with themes that fit the liturgical and calendar
year. Our priest popped in regularly to visit and offer his insights
on the topic of the month. At our first gathering, we welcomed a
lot of our regular daytime crowd but also several new faces. One
woman was a doctor who saw patients during the workday. Two
newcomers were active-duty army officers. Another woman,
whose first language was Spanish, also attended. Our gathering
was small but steady.

We were especially excited that two service members participated, reaping immediate results from our efforts to put into
action our refrain of "We should reach out." However, as the
months went on, they stopped coming. One did not want to part
from her young child during those coveted pre-bedtime hours.
The other woman, Kelley, sent us a gracious email when she left
the group. Kelley thanked us for welcoming her but shared that
she and several other active-duty women had started their own
Bible study that met in their offices. She felt better connected
with that group. We saw each other at church on Sundays and
stayed in touch, and in the months to come, as new active-duty
women arrived in the community, I invited them to the book
club but put them in touch with Kelley as well. Most of these
women connected with the active-duty gathering.

Though our efforts to bring active-duty women into the
mostly military spouse women's ministry fell flat, we were faithful in going to this population. We were successful, however, in a
way that we did not anticipate. We discovered that our book club
attracted international women. Our Spanish-speaking friend,
Marisol, who attended the book club monthly, shared that some
of the international women preferred this small gathering to the

larger daytime Bible study because they felt more comfortable speaking English in the more intimate setting.

Just as the ladies in the book club reached out to Marisol with a personal invitation, she, in turn, invited others, including her college-age daughter, who began sharing new titles with the group. Within a few months, our daytime gathering of mostly stay-at-home moms had established a lively evening book club comprising women from a wide range of ages and life experiences: nineteen to fifty, stay-at-home moms and working women, married and single, and women from several countries. Together we bonded through books and conversation, and that blessing endured in the form of Christ-centered friendships that continue ten years later, even though all of us had moved to different installations or retired from military life.

APPLY
STUCK IN YOUR COMFORT ZONE?

In an established women's ministry such as the daytime Bible study that I enjoyed when I was a stay-at-home mom, it can sometimes be a challenge to remember to reach out, because we get comfortable in our own gatherings and enjoy the familiarity. However, if our women's ministry gatherings do not reach out evangelistically, we miss opportunities to share the faith with women who may not have the same schedules, family structures, career paths, socioeconomic status, or first language as we do. We risk making a women's ministry cliquish or unapproachable, or ignoring women who long to know the gift of God but, for whatever reason, do not "gather at the well" with the established ministry group.

Women's ministries must nurture a missionary spirit to share the Gospel message beyond the confines of the group. As you work to cultivate that spirit, spend some time with the Samaritan woman at Jacob's well.

Getting Started

The story of the woman at the well is the longest one-on-one dialogue recorded between Jesus and any other person, and there is immense richness to glean from its text. As John recorded, the story begins at about noon. This detail is significant because women would have gathered at the well in the mornings or in the evenings but not in the height of the midday heat. Some surmise that the woman went to the well at noon because she was not accepted by the other women in her community. By drawing water at the height of the day, she could avoid confrontation or ridicule from women whose sins were less obvious.

Jesus braves the heat and meets the woman just as she is. "Give me a drink," he tells her (Jn 4:7). Since Jews did not share anything in common with Samaritans, his directive is shocking because drinking from the Samaritan woman's cup would entail sharing with someone ritualistically impure under Jewish teaching. I imagine that the woman, who was already downtrodden, reflexively presumed that Jesus was mocking her low status. She was, after all, the Hester Prynne of John's gospel—albeit without the scarlet letter.

When I consider her response—"How can you, a Jew, ask me, a Samaritan woman, for a drink?" (Jn 4:9)—I perceive anger, a smack of attitude, and spurn. I imagine that she ached to retreat to her home, where she would be sheltered from the unrelenting heat and further ridicule. But Jesus pursues her, "If you knew the gift of God and who is saying to you, 'Give me a drink,' you would have asked him and he would have given you living water" (Jn 4:10). And, "Whoever drinks the water I shall give will never thirst; the water I shall give will become in him a spring of water welling up to eternal life" (Jn 4:14). Her interest piqued, the Samaritan tells Jesus, "Sir, give me this water, so that I may not be thirsty or have to keep coming here to draw water" (Jn 4:15).

Notice that, as Jesus draws her into conversation, he does not immediately reveal his truth to her. Instead he tests her: "Go call your husband and come back" (Jn 4:16). I think he is probing to see if she is willing to be honest with him, because after all, a relationship starts with honesty. With his request, the woman's mask, which only lightly veiled her past deeds, shatters. Disarmed, she confesses, "I do not have a husband." Jesus responds, "You are right in saying, 'I do not have husband.' For you have had five husbands, and the one you have now is not your husband" (Jn 4:17–18).

In his candid truth-telling, the woman recognizes Jesus as a prophet: "I know that the Messiah is coming, the one called the Anointed; when he comes, he will tell us everything" (Jn 4:25). I imagine that while speaking, she raised a suspicious eyebrow, brimming with women's intuition that asked, "Are you the Messiah?" Why else would Jesus then tell her, "I am he, the one who is speaking with you" (Jn 4:26)?

After having this personal encounter, the Samaritan did what all women in ministry should do: she went to the townspeople with the evangelistic spirit of a missionary disciple and shared the gift of God, proclaiming, "Come see a man who told me everything I have done. Could he possibly be the Messiah?" (Jn 4:29). The people left the town and encountered Jesus at the well for themselves.

John leaves some details out of this story. For example, to whom specifically did she go and point to the well? Did she run to other outcasts like herself, to offer encouragement? Or did she preach to the women who condemned her, bearing witness to Jesus' radical love for the least? Did she go to the five husbands of her past, to point them toward true love incarnate? Those details are lost to history. But no matter the cross section of society, these people were just like her five minutes earlier—they did not know the gift of God. But because of her witness, they do.

"Inreach" and Outreach: Areas of Opportunity for Ministry

As one of the first women in Christian ministry, the Samaritan demonstrates that women's ministry is not about gathering with women who look, act, and have the same social status or work schedules as we do. It is about sharing the gift of God and pointing *all* to Jesus, the well of living water.

The Samaritan woman shows us how to be courageous, to leave our places of safety—like the solitude of the well at midday—and go out to the townspeople. As she demonstrates, sharing our stories and our faith with others is how many people initially come to know God and become interested in encountering Jesus for themselves. As John shares, "Many of the Samaritans in the town initially believed in [Jesus] because of the word of the woman who testified, 'He told me everything I have done'" (Jn 4:39). But after encountering Jesus themselves, the townspeople shared their own conversions with the woman, "We no longer believe because of your word; for we have heard for ourselves, and we know that this is truly the savior of the world" (Jn 4:42).

Our call in women's ministry is the same as the Samaritan woman's: to take our experience of encountering Jesus—at prayer, in service, or through the ordinary moments of life—and share that encounter with others so that they, like the townspeople, come to know Jesus personally. This form of ministry can take two distinct forms, each with unique approaches.

The first form is *inreach*, attracting and drawing into the circle of ministry those from within the parish community who do not currently participate in your group. This is what Pope John Paul II referred to as the "New Evangelization," reaching and renewing the faith of those already in the pews who, for whatever reason, do not fully engage in the life of the Church.

The second form of ministry is *outreach*—that is, inviting people who are not currently a part of your parish. This could include neighbors and casual acquaintances, coworkers who express an interest in spiritual things, and others in your sphere of influence whom you encounter every day. Consider hosting a special event, such as a charitable benefit or family movie night, and extend personal invitations to those God lays upon your heart.

Who are the women in your pews who crave a deeper relationship with Jesus and would benefit from inreach? Who are the women outside of your parish who do not know the gift of God? Who are the women who long to grow in their faith but have not yet found a community in which to grow? Who would benefit from outreach? These are today's Samaritan women and townspeople. Pray for the desire to reach out, for opportunities to practice missionary discipleship, and for the courage to act when we recognize these opportunities.

St. Katharine Drexel, a Model for Missionary Discipleship

St. Katharine Drexel is a keen role model and intercessor for us as we respond to God's prompting to meet women at the well. Born in Philadelphia, Pennsylvania, in 1858, Katharine's parents raised her in a devoutly Catholic home where the faith permeated their lives.

Katharine's father built his fortune in the banking industry and gave generously to those in need, particularly to Catholic charities. When he died, his estate at that time was the largest probated in Philadelphia. Immediately, one-tenth of his fortune was distributed to religious charities and the remainder was put in trust for his three daughters.

Katharine continued her father's legacy of generosity. In 1885, Katharine funded the Bureau of Catholic Indian Missions to open a boarding school for Sioux Indians in South Dakota. She soon followed this with another donation to open a school for the Osage Indians in Oklahoma.

Katharine had the wealth and status to live a life of comfort and influence in Philadelphia social circles. However, she discerned that God had other plans for her. Like the woman at the well, she was called to be a missionary among the most marginalized minority groups of her time. In 1887, as she discerned her vocation to religious life, Katharine visited Rome and attended a private audience with Pope Leo XIII, where she asked the Holy Father to send missionary priests to the Indians. He responded, "Why not, my child, yourself become a missionary?"[1] So she did.

In 1889, she traded the ball gowns and expensive millinery of Philadelphia society for the robes and veil of religious life as she entered the novitiate of the Sisters of Mercy in Pittsburgh. On February 12, 1891, she became the first professed sister of the community she established, the Sisters of the Blessed Sacrament for Indians and Colored People. Katharine's decision to bring the gift of God to "the least of these" rocked Philadelphia social circles. One newspaper headline announced her decision as "Miss Drexel Gives up Seven Million!"[2] Katharine was resolute.

By 1894, Katharine opened her first mission in Santa Fe, New Mexico, for the Pueblo Indians, who were at the time completely unschooled. By 1899, she opened St. Francis de Sales School in Powhatan, Virginia, for African American girls, and in short order, she worked with the Cincinnati Province of Franciscans to open St. Michael Indian School in Arizona, arranging for the friars to take over the school once the sisters moved to new missions. Katharine had such a missionary spirit that she traveled nearly six months out of the year to assist and encourage her sisters, while always being vigilant of new opportunities to serve. Through one visit, Katharine perceived the need to better catechize the Navajo children in their native tongue, so she oversaw the funding, translation, and printing of a Navajo-English catechism.

In 1925, seeing the need to provide higher education for African Americans in Louisiana, she founded Xavier University of Louisiana to educate African American teachers who would work in the racially segregated schools. Her legacy is clearly visible in the New Orleans school system, where a study conducted in 1987 found that nearly 40 percent of teachers in the public school system were Xavier alumni.

Like the Samaritan woman at the well, Katharine was compelled to share Jesus' message, and any fear of rejection that she may have felt could not restrain her missionary spirit. In Nashville, during the height of segregation and racism that plagued the South, Katharine persisted in opening a school for African American girls. Even when white landowners would not sell her property on which to open the school, she persevered creatively and conducted real-estate transactions through third-party businessmen, who, in turn, conveyed the property to her religious order. She was relentless in serving the least and undeterred by bullies. Imagine if we all served the Church with such courage!

As times evolved through the 1950s, *Brown v. Board of Education* finally overruled the "separate but equal" doctrine of *Plessy v. Ferguson*, and Nashville's schools were integrated racially. Katharine and her sisters closed the girls' school in Nashville, but their mission to serve these girls did not change. Katharine's sisters funded sending the girls to the racially integrated Catholic high school.

Katharine died in 1955, at the age of ninety-six. Today, the Sisters of the Blessed Sacrament continue to minister in the United States and abroad and promote social justice, particularly for the poor and vulnerable.

A common thread between the woman at the well, St. Katharine Drexel, today's Sisters of the Blessed Sacrament, and my women's ministry book club is the instinctive nature to share the Good News with others. This instinct imbues our ministries' work with an evangelistic spirit.

Who Are You Currently Reaching?

As you cultivate a missionary spirit in your women's ministry, consider who you currently serve, and where new opportunities for community outreach (or inreach within your own parish) might be. Below is a broad list of descriptive aspects of women you may serve. Does your women's ministry currently serve women who are:

Millennials?
Stay-at-home moms?
Single?
Married?
Immigrants or refugees?
Working professionals?
Members of the military?
Discerning religious
    vocations?
Recovering from
    abortion?
Preparing for marriage?
Divorced or separated?
Victims of domestic
    violence or abusive
    relationships?

Marginalized?
Non-Catholic?
Non-Christian?
Single mothers?
Adoptive parents?
Foster parents?
Widows?
Disabled?
Caregivers to aging
    parents?
Moms of special-needs
    children?
Grandmothers?
Terminally ill?
Homeless?

Who Are You Underserving?

Considering the list on the previous page, who are your underserving? How can you reach out to share the gift of God with these women and point them toward Jesus? As you consider how to reach out, be realistic. One of the challenges in women's ministry is balancing our generous hearts with acknowledging that we cannot do everything. The woman at the well began her missionary work with a first step: going to the townspeople. St. Katharine's sisters began their work with Native Americans with a first mission in Santa Fe. Our little book club began with one gathering. Take one first step. Wouldn't you love to increase the joy of just one woman?

momentum builders

TIPS FOR MEETING WOMEN AT THE WELL

The following is a list of practical ways that your community might renew your outreach and inreach efforts to draw new women to the well of fellowship.

Tip #1. Renew the invitation. Constantly invite people to join the women's ministry in your parish. You can do this most effectively through a personal invitation or an announcement in the bulletin or on social media. Sometimes opportunities to extend an invitation crop up unexpectedly. Stay awake and be ready!

For example, one day I was having lunch at a local restaurant and editing this book. My server, Ursula, noted from reading over my shoulder that I was writing something Catholic. She shared that she used to be Catholic but had left the Church because she felt hurt by the Church during her divorce. Suddenly, she sat down at my table and started to cry. I did not know what to do but to say that I was sorry that she had been hurt. I invited her to the brand-new women's Bible study at my parish. I told her that I thought the women were very welcoming, and I gave her my phone number. I also reminded her that as a baptized Catholic, she was *still* Catholic and always welcome.

Two weeks later my phone rang. To my surprise, it was Ursula. She told me that she was thankful for the invitation but that she was not ready to come back yet. I let her know that she could call me anytime and to let me know if she changed her mind. I do not know the end of Ursula's story, and neither does she, but she knows she is invited.

Tip #2. Host a speaker or parish mission. Hosting a keynote speaker for an evening or weekend conference or retreat is a great way to reach out. People who do not normally attend the women's ministry may be attracted to hearing a notable speaker. If you can work with the pastor to pair the event with Mass or adoration, even better. Be sure to invite all who attend to join the established ministries in the parish.

Events can be great catalysts for conversion or reversion. My friend Brigid attended a talk about the Sacrament of Reconciliation and invited her Catholic friend, Susan, to join her. After the talk, priests were available for Reconciliation. Brigid and Susan lined up for Reconciliation together. Susan later surprised Brigid, telling her that it was her first confession in decades! Between the event, the invitation, and the sacraments, Susan was brought back to the fullness of grace.

Tip #3. Listen to the "we shoulds." Pay attention when people say, "We should." My ministry group collectively said, "We should reach out to active-duty women." The woman at the well knew that she *should* run to the townspeople to share the gift of God. Katharine Drexel felt a calling in her heart that she *should* share the message of God with Native Americans and African Americans.

These inner feelings and verbal expressions of "we should" often reveal to us the people whom God is asking us to serve.

Consider how often you hear things such as the following:

◦ "We should serve at the soup kitchen."

◦ "We should have a resource for moms with kids with special needs."

◦ "We should make gift baskets for the parish staff at Christmas."

Women share these ideas because they have sensed a need to extend charity to feed the hungry, encourage families with special-needs children, increase fellowship between the women, or express gratitude. What we really *must* do is change our "We should" into "We shall."

Tip #4. Don't feel compelled to do everything. If you are a ministry leader and your community has expressed a need to serve in a new way, this does not mean that *you* are the person to make the new endeavor happen. Reaching out in a new way is an opportunity to inspire people to step up and "get a little skin in the game." St. Katharine initially started missions for Native Americans; however, once each mission was established, she relied on another religious community to continue to run the mission. She and her sisters often moved on to start new missions.

When I lived in Texas, our ministry group wanted to reach out to the local pro-life pregnancy center and offer support through donated items. Our faith-study group gathered baby items to donate, and I arranged a time to meet with the center's staff to deliver the items and take a tour. During our visit, the staff members expressed that they needed volunteers to sort the baby pantry, which was a place where parents could obtain clothes, diapers, and formula at no cost. They also needed on-site help to greet guests at their annual gala dinner.

As I listened, I felt guilt creeping up. The center needed help, but I did not have any more time in my schedule for additional service. However, several other women in the ministry group had time to give. I learned a lesson that day, and I continue to relearn it regularly: As women's ministry leaders, we can create opportunities for our community to spread the Gospel message without feeling obligated to lead or participate in every single opportunity. It is okay not to do it all!

If your women's ministry offers an opportunity for women to reach out, and it is successful—great. If not, as St. Katharine Drexel told her sisters, the mission is not to be successful; the mission is to be faithful.[3] Your women's ministry may feel called to take large leaps to evangelize the Gospel, as did St. Katharine, who went to Santa Fe. Or you may feel called to evangelize by incrementally creating more opportunities for women in the parish to participate in Bible studies or book groups. The important thing is that your ministry fosters the missionary spirit of the woman at the well.

PONDER

Today's passage to ponder is from the Gospel of John (4:27–42), which captures the moments as the disciples return to find the Samaritan woman with Jesus. Read the passage slowly and prayerfully before answering the questions below.

> At that moment his disciples returned, and were amazed that he was talking with a woman, but still no one said, "What are you looking for?" or "Why are you talking with her?" The woman left her water jar and went into the town and said to the people, "Come see a man who told me everything I have done. Could he possibly be the Messiah?" They went out of the town and came to him.

Meanwhile, the disciples urged him, "Rabbi, eat."
But he said to them, "I have food to eat of which
you do not know." So the disciples said to one another, "Could someone have brought him something
to eat?" Jesus said to them, "My food is to do the
will of the one who sent me and to finish his work.
Do you not say, 'In four months the harvest will be
here'? I tell you, look up and see the fields ripe for the
harvest. The reaper is already receiving his payment
and gathering crops for eternal life, so that the sower
and reaper can rejoice together. For here the saying
is verified that 'One sows and another reaps.' I sent
you to reap what you have not worked for; others
have done the work, and you are sharing the fruits
of their work."

Many of the Samaritans of that town began to
believe in him because of the word of the woman who
testified, "He told me everything I have done." When
the Samaritans came to him, they invited him to stay
with them; and he stayed there two days. Many more
began to believe in him because of his word, and they
said to the woman, "We no longer believe because of
your word; for we have heard for ourselves, and we
know that this is truly the savior of the world."

1. Read the passage again as an exercise in *lectio divina*, or
    "spiritual reading." This involves reading the passage several
    times—you might want to do this exercise in adoration or
    before the tabernacle, where Jesus is present. The first time,
    simply read the passage and pay attention to any details or
    words that jump out at you. What might God be saying to
    you through his Word? Read the passage again, and this time
    write down your thoughts about this passage. Finally, read
    the passage slowly and then spend time in silent contempla-
    tion, just letting God speak to you. Allow at least twenty to
    thirty minutes to complete this exercise. After completing

the exercise, share your experience and insights with your ministry group or a friend in ministry.

2. How has someone reached out to help you come to know Jesus? What did that person do? How did the invitation make you feel?

3. Who are the "women at the well" in your community? They may not be outcast, but they are definitely underserved. What are three concrete steps your community could take to reach out to them?

4. What are the "we shoulds" in your community or in your heart? What *should* you do about them? Have you ever felt or verbalized a "we should" in your community? How did you respond to it?

Closing Prayer

Lord, you met the woman at the well at the height of the day, Katharine Drexel in the comfort of her home, and us exactly where we are in life. As we come to know you as the Living Water, ignite in us the zeal of missionary disciples. Grant us the awareness to recognize opportunities to reach out and the courage to do so. Amen.

6

Return to Draw Water:

PRACTICING ASSESSMENT

> If we wish to serve God and love
> our neighbor well, we must mani-
> fest our joy in the service we render
> to Him and them. Let us open wide
> our hearts. It is joy which invites us.
> Press forward and fear nothing.
> —St. Katharine Drexel

SHARE

Nestled in the foothills of the German Alps, you will find Ettal Abbey, an imposing, fourteenth-century Benedictine abbey whose intricately gilded baroque architecture sharply contrasts the surrounding bucolic landscape. The first time I visited the European continent, I traveled to Ettal to speak at a Catholic women's conference for the military archdiocese. I took an overnight flight from Houston, Texas, to Munich, Germany, before boarding a train to Garmisch, Bavaria, in southern Germany, where my friend Jane, the retreat organizer, met me.

As the train lumbered out of Munich's central terminal, the gray cityscape of post–World War II urban concrete reconstruction faded into centuries-old villages, where onion-domed church steeples peaked over the sharply angled, wooden roofs of Bavaria. Only cows, buttercups, and wayside crucifixes populated the pastures between each village. The crucifixes, I later learned, serve as midday shrines for herders and farmers.

When Jane met me at the train station, I was exhausted to the point of dizziness, and I nearly fell asleep in the front passenger seat en route to the abbey. Thankfully I did not. As we climbed a mountain and rounded a bend, Jane said, "Now look to your right." I was dumbstruck. Ettal Abbey was the most majestic edifice I had ever seen. Its gleaming chapel dome towered over the tree line, five times higher than any other structure in the village.

I had a good night's rest in a local guesthouse and went for a walk in the village the next morning before the start of the retreat. Ettalers greeted me with "*Gruss gott*"—"God bless you"—the Bavarian manner of saying good morning. Ettal is infused with the Catholic faith. Church bells ring five minutes before Masses and Benedictine prayer times (at least during the day), and street signs caution drivers to slow down for pedestrians crossing to the abbey. Life in Ettal ticks to the meter of the Benedictine Rule, beckoning locals and tourists alike.

When the retreat began, nearly 150 American women from US military installations in Europe—Italy, Spain, Belgium, England, and Germany—congregated at the abbey anticipating a peaceful weekend of prayer, liturgies, spiritual talks, and fellowship with friends.

As with many women's ministries, this annual retreat has developed several closely held traditions over the years. One tradition is prayer sisters, which encourages women to meet new people by praying for one another. For prayer sisters, every woman fills out a card with special prayer requests at the beginning of the weekend and leaves her card in a basket. Another woman draws her card and prays especially for her. Throughout the weekend, women leave notes and small gifts for their prayer sisters, and at the end of the retreat, the women reveal their prayer sisters to one another. It is a sweet way for women from different communities to connect, and it makes our geographically dispersed archdiocese feel a little bit smaller.

Another time-honored tradition is a silent auction that raises money to pay for the seminary tuition of men studying to become Catholic chaplains. From time in memoriam, the silent auction has involved placing gift baskets donated by the women and bid sheets around the retreat's main meeting room. Women bid on the baskets during breaks or at the conclusion of each day's activities. On the last day of the retreat, the highest bidders win the baskets, and the retreat leaders proudly announce how much the women raised. With 150 ladies in attendance, it is not uncommon for these auctions to raise between $8,000 and $10,000. The women love supporting the seminarians.

Over time, however, the silent auction increasingly began to resemble a street bazaar. In addition to the baskets, women brought smaller items to raffle—used books, tea towels, handicrafts, cheese plates, German beer steins, Polish pottery—you name it! There were hundreds of things to bid on or win.

I love a good seminarian fundraiser as much as the next Catholic woman, but we realized that this tradition was out of hand when some women began leaving the spiritual talks to stalk their bid sheets and guard the most coveted baskets. This was monumentally distracting, and the women who organized the retreat were upset that the zealous bidders had missed the thoughtful presentations. "We are selling goods on the Temple steps!" declared an irate woman; she was ready to take a page from Jesus' playbook and start turning over tables.

In the midst of the medieval abbey, where prayer and worship had dictated each day's rhythm for centuries, the cacophony of bidding had stifled the speakers' words and dampened the pealing bells calling all to prayer. The women who lovingly began the silent auction so many years before had not foreseen this development. Clearly something had to be done.

At the retreat's end, the leadership decided to refocus the retreat to its principal purposes: spiritual growth and formation. In the weeks that followed, they discussed foregoing the auction at the next retreat and simply taking up a collection for the seminarians at one of the Masses. However, women loved creating their gift baskets and shopping during the retreat, and we all acknowledged that the auction brought fun and enthusiasm to the fundraiser in a way that passing an offering plate could not replicate.

In the end, the leadership team decided to scale back the silent auction at future retreats, limiting it in both time and location. On the last night of the retreat, when the leadership hosted a plated banquet dinner, women were given one hour immediately before the banquet to bid on baskets, and at the conclusion of the dinner, the retreat leaders enthusiastically announced the winners. One of the retreat leaders even dressed up in a ball gown and did her best Vanna White impression as she delivered items to winners.

The organizers also added a live auction to the banquet to fundraise with those smaller items that the women loved to donate. Excited women shouted out their bids and cheered each other on. At one point, to our surprise, our priest took the microphone and assumed auctioneer duties. The evening was a hit. Those who did not participate in the bidding were still able to support the seminarians through an offering collected at the weekend's closing Mass.

The adjustments preserved the intent of seminarian support and still raised about the same amount for the seminarians. Everyone agreed that the banquet and shorter auction eliminated the distractions, and for the most part, the retreatants were happy about the new format. The planners balanced the aspects that the women loved about the traditional silent auction, and there was still time for shopping, bidding, winning, and supporting the seminarians. In addition, the women enjoyed the dressy dinner.

However, their sincere efforts still encountered some criticism. Since the old format was well-established, several women lamented that we had disregarded tradition. A few women felt put on the spot to make bids at the live auction when it was already a significant financial expense to register for the retreat. Of course, no amount of explanation could draw in complete support. In the end, the retreat planners had to take heart that they did their best to improve upon an important tradition.

APPLY

This silent auction experience underscores three important aspects of adjusting or revising a women's ministry tradition:

1. *Take time to assess both the overall ministry as well as individual programs and other offerings, especially before making a major change.* Looking back, it is no surprise that over time the auction grew out of hand. Very gradually and incrementally, the event grew from a contained bidding process on one gift basket per chapel community, to auctioning and raffling off many offerings throughout the entire retreat. Those in leadership did not assess the auction process and results at the conclusion of each retreat, or they did not heed or implement feedback. If they had, the leaders would have been able to make incremental adjustments years ago, rather than jarring the community with a significant overhaul.

2. *Acknowledge that adjusting an established practice can be both difficult and necessary.* We have seen a lot of changes in the Church in the United States in recent years, from parish mergers, to improved screening and training for those who work with children and youth, to using digital media as a powerful way to

draw people into the faith. These changes are important, but can you think of any parish that unanimously celebrated a closure or merger, flocked to complete additional training and background checks, or embraced new technology? Of course not! In revising a ministry, expect some resistance, and remember Paul's encouragement to the Thessalonians, "Do not be remiss in doing good" (2 Thes 3:13).

3. *Proceed with humility.* Affirm and appreciate what is good, and act to enhance the ministry's work of pointing women toward a closer relationship with Jesus. After all, women's ministry programs are almost always born from volunteers' efforts to express their love of God through serving their neighbors. Assessment or adjustments should never be used to condemn or criticize others' efforts. We must respect the efforts of those who came before us and give cherished traditions careful attention. Keep in mind that soon your initiative may be a tradition, and you will want it to be revised with the same care that you poured into it. Do unto others.

Assessing and Affecting Change

Assessing and adjusting ministry work is not unique to parish or lay women's ministry. Recall that St. Katharine Drexel and her Sisters of the Blessed Sacrament had to make significant adjustments to their work, such as closing the high school for African American girls in Nashville in the 1950s and sending the students to the racially integrated Catholic high school.

In 2015, the community also had to make significant changes, including closing the National Shrine of St. Katharine Drexel in Bensalem, Pennsylvania, and putting the property up for sale. In 2018, Katharine's body was transferred from the shrine that was built with great care, to her childhood church, the Cathedral Basilica of Saints Peter and Paul, in downtown Philadelphia. These decisions were not taken lightly, but they were the right decisions to ensure that the sisters could continue their good work and place Katharine's remains in repose where they can be venerated and her legacy remembered.

This chapter outlines a method for building assessment into a ministry to help you make adjustments incrementally. These assessments are useful whether you are evaluating the overall effectiveness of the ministry (perhaps in preparation for the upcoming year) or the success of a particular program or initiative. It can be tempting to move immediately to the next project without assessing our work or leaving notes or continuity files for those who take the reins for the next iteration. (More on continuity files in chapter 8.) However, if we fail to assess, we forfeit the opportunity to improve.

—momentum builders—
SURVEYS FOR LEADERSHIP AND PARTICIPANTS

An effective assessment involves gathering and interpreting feedback not only from the leadership team, including your pastor, but also from those in the parish community. To begin assessment, first reach out to the current leadership and the pastor for self-assessment. Each person on the leadership team should take some time to answer a Women's Ministry Leader Survey (see note on next page).

Next, circulate a Women's Ministry Participant Survey to women in the parish. I recommend completing the surveys using an online survey tool or app, so that you can share the results by email and social media, track responses, replicate, and store the survey to compare data periodically. If you use paper surveys, be sure that someone will aggregate and share the responses in a meaningful way, so that feedback does not end up collecting dust in a ministry closet in the parish hall. To ensure participation, give women time to complete the surveys during a ministry gathering.

Note: Free, downloadable versions of both surveys are available at joyfulmomentum.org and avemariapress.com.

Interpreting Surveys and Implementing Change

Once the ministry group has completed the surveys, the leadership team should take time to review the feedback to interpret the results. It can be helpful for the team to have a mini-retreat to complete this work. Begin the retreat with Mass or prayer time before jumping into the survey. Celebrate the beautiful aspects of your work. Dedicate time to discuss:

- Trends in the surveys
- Areas where the ministry is strong
- Areas where there is room for improvement
- Surprising responses
- Adjustments to current work based on feedback

After you have interpreted the surveys and identified any needed adjustments, chart the way ahead. Change can be challenging, so first consider quick adjustments you can make that will not involve disturbing near-and-dear traditions. Then consider whether the ministry needs to make more significant adjustments.

For example, once the women's ministry in Europe completed and incorporated a meaningful assessment of the Ettal retreat, they learned that the women loved the "prayer sisters" tradition and that it was helping the women connect with one another. They also learned something unexpected: retreatants wanted to go to Confession in their native language. An easy way to address this was to find a Spanish-speaking priest and a German-speaking priest for the next retreat's penance service. This might not have helped the women whose first language was Vietnamese, but it was a simple way to be inclusive and make the sacraments more available. Without taking time to listen to the feedback, the leadership team would not have known of the need for additional languages.

If your ministry decides to pursue more holistic revisions, put the plan down on paper and chart out benchmarks on a calendar. Meet with the pastor to propose the plan and communicate how you came to this conclusion. It can be valuable to publish or discuss with the ministry group the survey results or themes that led to the decision. If your ministry publishes the survey results, thank the participants and explain in a few main points how the leadership is incorporating the feedback into the ministry. This will help build trust and buy-in within the ministry. As you communicate the ministry team's intent, invite others to join the effort. This will help recruit new leaders and afford everyone an opportunity to serve with their spiritual gifts.

St. Katharine Drexel, a Model for Prayerful Change

It is vitally important that in the process of assessing any ministry, prayer remains at the heart of the discussion. This was modeled effectively by St. Katharine Drexel, who wrote, "If I can say of an action, 'I did it out of love of God,' there is something about it that will last through all eternity."[1]

As you implement this assessment process, consider making a novena (a nine-day prayer) with your leadership team. The novena of St. Katharine Drexel, which may be found at katharinedrexel.org, focuses on some of the most important facets of women's ministry: Eucharist, evangelization, peace, kindness, suffering, the Cross, devotion to Mary, building for eternity, and prayer and work.[2] Ask St. Katharine to pray that your team would rightly discern God's will for the ministry and have the courage to follow where he is leading the group.

―momentum builders―
TIPS FOR ADJUSTING ESTABLISHED TRADITIONS

If assessing the ministry reveals that it is time to adjust an established tradition, tread carefully but deliberately. Here are three tips to help you through this process.

Tip #1. Take time to discern whether the tradition needs to be revised or eliminated. Unless the tradition is harmful, I recommend trying to revise a tradition before eliminating it, because the women who built the tradition do not want their work tossed aside.

Tip #2. Involve tradition stakeholders as well as the pastor and newcomers in the changes. Be prepared for pushback and to explain the rationale for changing a tradition. As you assess the feedback from the group, be prepared to revise your work further, or even revert to the previous practices.

Tip #3. Always proceed with humility. While proponents of revising a program or tradition may believe they are righteously tipping a fattened calf, the women who have nurtured a tradition over the years may perceive the efforts like Solomon's threat to cut a baby in half. Tread graciously and remember that the ultimate aim of change is to be more effective at pointing women to Jesus.

─────────────────────────────

Through undertaking significant change in the school in Nashville in the 1950s, and again between 2015 and 2018 in closing St. Katharine's shrine, the Sisters of the Blessed Sacrament adjusted their work to better accomplish their mission to share the Gospel with the poor. Though these decisions were not always easy, they kept God's call on the community at the forefront of their work. In our women's ministries, we can be confident that prayerful, thoughtful, and humble actions to improve a ministry will help us continue to serve as God has called us.

PONDER

Today's passage to ponder is from the Gospel of John (15:1–4, 9–17):

> "I am the true vine, and my Father is the vine grower. He takes away every branch in me that does not bear fruit, and every one that does he prunes so that it bears more fruit. You are already pruned because of the word that I spoke to you. Remain in me, as I remain in you. Just as a branch cannot bear fruit on its own unless it remains on the vine, so neither can you unless you remain in me. . . . As the Father loves me, so I also love you. Remain in my love. If you keep my commandments, you will remain in my love, just as I have kept my Father's commandments and remain in his love.
>
> "I have told you this so that my joy may be in you and your joy may be complete. This is my commandment: love one another as I love you. No one

has greater love than this, to lay down one's life for one's friends. You are my friends if you do what I command you. I no longer call you slaves, because a slave does not know what his master is doing. I have called you friends, because I have told you everything I have heard from my Father. *It was not you who chose me, but I who chose you and appointed you to go and bear fruit that will remain,* so that whatever you ask the Father in my name he may give you. This I command you: love one another."

1. As you read today's passage, think about how you bear fruit for God, the Vine Grower. How has God pruned you so that you can be more fruitful? Looking closely at the italicized text from verse 16, how has God caused your women's ministry to bear fruit?
2. Describe some family traditions. How do these bring joy to your life?
3. Now think of some traditions in your women's ministry. How do they increase joy in your community? How do these traditions enhance the mission? If your parish is starting a women's ministry, are there any traditions you would like to establish?
4. Does your parish or women's ministry currently assess its work and implement the feedback? If so, what have you learned, and what has surprised you about these assessments?
5. Have you ever resisted (or experienced resistance to) a change that you needed to make in life? How did you overcome the resistance?

Closing Prayer

Ever-loving God, you called St. Katharine Drexel to share the message of the Gospel and the life of the Eucharist with the poor and oppressed. As her community discerned how to continue to serve you through changing environments and across diverse populations, help us respond to changing needs in our communities. Guide us to seek and submit to your will. Through the intercession of St. Katharine Drexel, may we grow in the faith and love that will enable us to be united in ministry. Amen.

7

Go to Your Sister:

RESOLVING CONFLICT WITH MERCY

I demand from you deeds of mercy,
which are to arise out of love for
Me. You are to show mercy to your
neighbors always and everywhere.
You must not shrink from this or try
to excuse or absolve yourself from it.
—Jesus to St. Faustina Kowalska,
Diary, 742

SHARE

In a recent brainstorming session with a ministry group, our moderator tasked us to share ideas for creative projects. We were not to consider whether we *should* undertake these projects; we were just bouncing around ideas. No idea was too outlandish. I was encouraged by the participants' creativity and positivity. However, as the brainstorming progressed, a woman who had been involved for decades kept interrupting whoever was speaking with declarative statements such as "We've already done that" or "We tried that, but it didn't work."

When she interrupted me, I stopped speaking and shot daggers at the moderator, hoping that she would redirect the conversation. Unfortunately, telepathy is not one of my superpowers, and it became clear that open brainstorming was not possible.

So, there we were, twelve competent ministry leaders tolerating the interruptions. Why? Because we were conflict avoiders. That's right—conflict avoiders. How often do small conflicts like this erupt in women's ministry, or in life, for that matter? All. The. Time.

Finally I said to the moderator, "I think we have done enough for today. Perhaps we can submit our ideas in writing and regroup later." With that, our brainstorming ceased. We dispersed from the conference room, and I retreated to my workspace incensed because this latest round of interruptions was just one in a habitual series. That evening I stewed in annoyance about this woman's persistent interrupting. Then I stewed that nobody did anything about it. Then I stewed about being annoyed that I was stewing. I simmered away in my personal pressure cooker!

The next morning my agitation waned, and I called the moderator to talk about the issue. I affirmed that brainstorming was a good idea and acknowledged that the interrupting participant had a lot of experience and that I felt frustrated by the interruptions. I asked the moderator to consider passing the "speaking baton" or setting an order of who speaks, so that everyone could share ideas but also so that the other participants could listen to one another. The moderator agreed, and the subsequent conversations were far more productive.

Looking back, I doubt that the woman realized how off-putting and irritating her behavior had been. In fact, she was probably unaware that she was interrupting. Looking at the situation from her perspective, she was enthusiastic about sharing her knowledge and may have thought she was saving the group from wasting time on futile ideas.

I realize now that I might have resolved my conflict with this person by saying simply, "I understand you have something to share. Please give me a minute. I'm not finished yet, and I want you to be able to respond to my complete thought." This might have nipped the behavior. Alternatively, I could have asked the moderator to indicate who had the floor and who was next to speak. Either action might have helped allow a fruitful conversation. Instead, the group collectively tolerated the behavior, and as a result, we forfeited the opportunity to have a productive exchange of ideas.

APPLY
CONFLICT AND DIVERSITY

God creates tremendous diversity—from Mount Everest to Death Valley; from snails to elephants. God even created the diverse languages of the world. Diversity goes beyond the physical. He gifts some people as artists and others as mathematicians. We have diverse thoughts, values, methods of processing information, personalities, life experiences, and God-given charisms. God delights in our diversity. We know that perfect love can exist in diversity because we experience it in the Holy Trinity.

Getting Started

As much as God loves diversity, we see that the evil one often twists it, using it as a catalyst for strife and conflict. Conflict tends to occur at the intersection of diversity in all its forms. Scripture recounts numerous conflicts. Think of when the disciples argued about which one of them should be regarded as the greatest (see Luke 22:24), or when Mary and Martha experienced a conflict about serving their guests (see Luke 10:38–42). Cephas and Paul had such a conflict over hypocrisy that Paul rebuked Cephas: "I opposed him to his face because he clearly was wrong" (Gal 2:11). Paul went on to admonish the community at Galatia for straying from orthodox teaching: "Oh stupid Galatians! Who has bewitched you?" (Gal 3:1). Conflict is not necessarily bad or sinful. Sin often enters conflict when we choose to escalate a conflict or avoid resolving it. For example, a diversity of opinions about which Bible study to select in a women's ministry is not sinful at all. Thinking back to our ministry's frustrating brainstorming session, the woman's interruptions might have been accidental. But our responses, if rooted in pride, can embroil the conflict in sin. As Jesus warned, "What comes out of a person, that is what defiles" (Mk 7:20). Jesus specifically names several types of sin that we can be tempted to commit in response to conflict: evil thoughts, jealousy, envy, malice, deceit, or arrogance, among others (see Mark 7:21–22). If we resolve conflict with mercy, however, the process can help us grow in virtue and more united in community.

Taking Issue with Conflict

Some of us seem to feed on drama and relish conflict. Others avoid it at all costs—even if it means never reaching a peaceful resolution. Our reticence to resolve conflict reveals a striking paradox between how we safeguard our physical versus spiritual health.

When we are in physical pain, we visit the doctor or take medication. But when we experience the spiritual pain of interpersonal conflict, we let it gnaw at us—sometimes for years. I have personally felt the effect of unresolved conflict in my extended family, and it is excruciating and miserable.

Most of us choose not to resolve conflict for three main reasons.

1. *Concupiscence.* At some level, we like conflict because per-petuating it can make us feel so cozy with justification, self-righteousness, or personal affirmation.

2. *Spiritual cowardice.* Pursuing peaceful resolutions in con-flict takes spiritual courage. We prefer to be spiritual cowards because we are afraid to learn about our weaknesses or blind spots, to relive past hurts, to humble ourselves enough to listen to another person's perspective, to admit our own errors, and to let forgiveness and reconciliation mold us. We fear the fleeting pain of a Band-Aid ripping out a few arm hairs from our burly egos so much that we endure the pestilence of infection lurking in our souls. We allow interrupted conversations, hurt feelings, and insipid brooding instead of addressing the root cause of a conflict because conflict resolution is uncomfortable.

3. *Anemic conflict resolution skills.* We neglect to resolve con-flict because we do not know how. The good news is that if we can muster the gumption to step away from sin and claim a little spiritual courage, we can build this skill set. This chapter pro-vides a toolbox of strategies to resolve conflicts with mercy, with an eye toward resolution of the conflict, and toward forgiveness and reconciliation with God and all involved.

To resolve conflicts, we must recognize our role in conflict and make the conscious choice to stop using clever methods of perpetuating it. Unfortunately, some of these methods are habit-ual. You may be perpetuating conflict without even realizing it. But if we examine our behavior, we can take a first step toward conflict resolution.

How do you engage in conflict? Some people preserve con-flict by blowing up. Others huff away; some heave personal insults. Others give the silent treatment or banish like lepers the people with whom they disagree. And some flatly refuse to acknowledge the conflict at all! This stonewalling tactic ("What disagreement?" or "I'm not willing to discuss that!") removes any possibility of conflict resolution or reconciliation.

Another favorite method of escalating or avoiding conflict resolution is *triangulation*. This tactic can be so subtle you might be employing it without even realizing it. The term appears to have been coined by a psychiatrist at Georgetown University in the mid- to late-twentieth century. In its more noble form, triangulation is the tendency for two people in conflict to draw in a third person in hopes of easing the tension.[1] When Martha went to Jesus and said, "Lord, do you not care that my sister has left me by myself to do the serving? Tell her to help me" (Lk 10:40), she wanted Jesus to step in.

Similarly, in the example of the habitual interrupter, I called the moderator and asked her to lay ground rules for brainstorming so that I could avoid solving the conflict directly with the interrupter. In this limited situation, the triangulation may have been helpful because I did not step on the toes of the moderator publicly, but I also did not want to engage the interrupter directly.

However, very often we triangulate issues not to resolve conflict discretely but to avoid exercising *spiritual courage* or to invite others to take sides. This type of triangulation is glorified gossip, where the person drawing in the third party often plays the role of the victim, the third party is the rescuer, and the absent party is cast as the villain.[2]

Victim, rescuer, and villain may sound extreme, and if so—good! Because this behavior sows the seeds of discord in a community. If the third party allows it, the conflict becomes like sand in a bathing suit, irritating every part of us. It is so easy to slip into a pattern of triangulation because it can make us feel validated or vindicated. When I called the moderator about the interrupted conversation, at some level I was trying to triangulate the issue. I wanted the moderator to affirm my anger and commiserate with me. The moderator was wise enough not to engage.

Pope Francis said that "the father of division is the devil," and I believe that triangulation is one of the devil's favorite tools because it is so slippery.[3] We euphemize it with statements such as "I just need to vent," and then we tell a third party about how another person has done us wrong. You might also hear triangulation as "I'm not gossiping but . . ." In fact, you are *exactly* gossiping. You just gave it a flourishing overture. Sometimes we veil triangulation as a prayer request: "Please pray for me. I'm really struggling with Susie. Pray that she stops interrupting." Sure, the "victim" wants prayers because her feelings are hurt, but she also wants your commiseration about the "villain." A way to avoid this type of triangulation is just asking for a prayer for a personal intention or that God would heal a relationship. The prayer will be just as efficacious.

The Command to Love

We cannot afford to be conflict-avoiding cowards. We must build the spiritual courage to navigate conflicts, and we must start with the right baseline, which is that resolving conflict should be an exercise in perfecting love or charity. Charity is the theological virtue by which we love God above all things for his own sake, and our neighbor as ourselves for the love of God (*CCC* 1822). As Paul wrote, "So faith, hope, love abide, these three. But the greatest of these is love" (1 Cor 13:13). The *Catechism* substitutes "love" for "charity" in this famous Bible verse to stress that the Lord "asks us to love as he does" (*CCC* 1825).

Being charitable does not mean that we will never experience conflict or that we should be doormats for abusive behavior. In fact, charity demands balancing "beneficence and fraternal correction" (*CCC* 1829). Both are necessary. If we engage in conflict charitably, it can refine us, convert us, and increase our love and respect of our sisters in ministry. As we grow in charity, our relationships will more closely resemble the perfect love between the three persons of the Holy Trinity.

Resolving conflict with charity is not a choice; it is a command. Jesus commands us, "Love one another. As I have loved you, so you also should love one another. This is how all will know that you are my disciples, if you have love for one another" (Jn 13:34–35). The Greek word for love in this verse is *agape*, which is "selfless love," and the specific conjugation is *agapate*—it is a command, not a suggestion! First John expands: "Whoever loves his brother remains in the light," but "whoever hates his brother is in darkness; he walks in darkness and does not know where he is going because the darkness has blinded his eyes" (1 Jn 2:10–11). We must resolve conflict, therefore, with our eyes toward the light and a willingness to submit to Jesus' command to love selflessly.

---

momentum builders

TIPS TO RESOLVE CONFLICT WITH ANOTHER PERSON IN A MINISTRY

Avoidance is seldom the best way to resolve conflicts between two sisters in Christ. When you sense conflict is brewing, try to resolve it at the first sign of trouble by speaking directly with the other party. This is the golden rule of conflict: Go to your sister, not to inform her of what she has done wrong or how she has offended you. Be the first to make peace through acts of kindness and mercy. How? Let's take it step by step.

Tip #1. Invite her to talk. Explain to the other person that you want to discuss the conflict, and ask her to talk with you about it. Ask her to listen to you and express that you want to listen to her as well. Describe what you believe the conflict is and why. Ask her if she agrees with your assessment.

Tip #2. Use "I" statements. Focus on your feelings and impressions rather than her motivations. For example, "I felt unheard during the brainstorming session."

Tip #3. Affirm what is good about the other's behavior while also pointing out what is problematic. With the interrupter, I could have said, "I value that you have years of experience with these programs, and I am grateful for your wisdom. I ask you to make room for other people to share their ideas and experiences as well."

Tip #4. Find common ground by validating what you agree with. This helps narrow the conflict to specific acts or omissions rather than to a sweeping theme. You may find that you agree with a person's intentions but not her methods. That is something to affirm.

Tip #5. Discuss how to move forward. If, as Jesus says, "you win your sister over," then discuss how to prevent the same sort of conflict from happening again. With the interruptions, for example, we might agree to let each person finish speaking before the next person responds.

Tip #6. If you cannot find common ground, consider next steps. If speaking directly with the other party does not resolve the conflict, consider working with a disinterested person to seek resolution. Or perhaps God is nudging you to grow in humility and to bear the wrong patiently!

Tip #7. Refuse to let the issue create permanent damage or division between you. Continue to pray for God's blessing on the other person and ask God to soften your heart toward her. By refusing to gossip or escalate the conflict, you leave room for the Holy Spirit to work in both your hearts and to bring lasting peace and healing.

In the words of St. Paul, love "does not rejoice over wrongdoing but rejoices with the truth. It bears all things, believes all things, hopes all things, endures all things. Love never fails." (1 Cor 13:6–8).

St. Faustina Kowalska, a Model of Deeds, Words, and Prayers of Mercy

St. Maria Faustina Kowalska, who lived from 1905 to 1938, was a Polish nun and great mystic. She had an intimate relationship with Jesus in which he instructed her about his divine mercy through a series of prayers and dialogues. At Jesus' direction, Faustina recorded these conversations in her diary.

Jesus gave Faustina a way to live out the commandment to love one another by extending his mercy. He told her, "I demand from you deeds of mercy, which are to arise out of love for Me. You are to show mercy to your neighbors always and everywhere. You must not shrink from this or try to excuse or absolve yourself from it." Jesus continued, "I am giving you three ways of exercising mercy toward your neighbor: the first—by deed, the second—by word, the third—by prayer. In these three degrees is contained the fullness of mercy, and it is an unquestionable proof of love for Me."[4]

The instruction given to Faustina for extending God's mercy in all aspects of life can be our model for resolving conflicts as well. To resolve conflict, we must love those involved by extending mercy through our deeds, words, and prayers. If you are in a conflict but need an extra heaping of charity before you are ready to extend mercy, then take some time to look into your heart. Seek counsel from a spiritual director or spiritual friend, ask God to increase your charity. Go to the Sacrament of Reconciliation to receive the graces of forgiveness for your own actions before you engage with the other person. This will help you step away from the emotion and sin that are smoke screens to love and, instead, replace them with mercy that perfuses like incense. Even if you are not ready or able to offer deeds or words of mercy, Faustina wrote, "then pray—that too is mercy."[5]

Deeds, Words, and Prayers of Mercy

Conflict resolution can be hard work, but we must do it, because being reconciled is part of our path to holiness. Jesus told Faustina, "Know this, My daughter: if you strive for perfection you will sanctify many souls; and if you do not strive for sanctity, by the same token, many souls will remain imperfect."[6] If we look at resolving conflict as a collective work of mercy, we can appreciate how our deeds, words, and prayers can affect the whole community. They form a testament to our love of God.

The following is a list of methods to extend merciful deeds, words, and prayers to resolve conflicts.

1. *Identify the conflict—what it is and what it is not.* When we experience conflict, our emotions career in all kinds of directions, and we can be tempted to respond to what we currently feel rather than the actual conflict. If a conflict has dragged on for a long time with lots of triangulated conversations, lost tempers, or harm to others, it may be difficult to identify what the original conflict was versus the secondary and tertiary ripples.

As a deed of mercy, ask God to help you strip away the drama and reveal the root of the conflict. You may realize that a conflict is not actually a conflict and move on. You may find that the conflict is real and that you need to pursue reconciliation. When I was upset about the person interrupting me, I spiraled into being angry about a time the woman had hurt my feelings nearly a decade earlier. It took some time to peel back years of interactions and emotions to realize that the conflict was simple:

I wanted to be heard, and I wanted to listen to what others had to say; the interrupting prevented that. My anger about past wrongs occluded the current issue.

2. *Seek counsel.* If the conflict is particularly sticky, you may need to seek counsel from a trusted friend or spiritual director—someone with whom you share one of the foundational relationships that we talked about in chapter 1—to drill down to the actual conflict. This is a deed of mercy because it will help ready your heart and mind to address the conflict. It is okay to seek genuine counsel from someone who is not attached to or embroiled in the conflict, and who will offer advice without allowing you to drag them in or triangulate the issue. When you seek counsel, describe your perspective and ask the person to help you see the other person's view, how you might be even contributing to the issue, or if there is a "wooden beam" in your eye (Mt 7:5).

3. *Bear wrongs patiently.* Have you ever heard the phrase "Bless and release?" To bless and release is when you pray for the situation, forgive it, and let it go from your mind. In more theological terms, this is the spiritual work of mercy of bearing wrongs patiently. Sometimes in conflict we realize that we are willing to bear a wrong and "offer it up." In my conflict with the interrupter, I decided to accept this impulsiveness, forgive it, and ask God to increase my patience—bless and release. I did not condone the interrupting, but I decided to bear it patiently.

St. Faustina displayed heroic virtue in her ability to bear wrongs patiently. One time, when she left the chapel at her convent, an antagonistic sister said to her sarcastically, "Sister, you want to be a saint? Pigs will fly before that'll happen." In the midst of this mean-spirited insult, Sr. Faustina responded, "Sister, I love you even more."[7] Offering these sorts of deeds and prayers of mercy are important spiritual exercises, especially if you have a knack for brooding.

4. *Go to your sister.* If after reflection you decide to address
a conflict, go directly to your sister and talk with her about it
(see the Momentum Builder section above). Jesus gives us the
example of how to extend this deed of mercy when the conflict
involves sin: "If your brother sins [against you], go and tell him
his fault between you and him alone. If he listens to you, you
have won over your brother" (Mt 18:15). Jesus advises us that if
your sister does not listen, then "take one or two others along
with you" (Mt 18:16). If you must resolve a sinful conflict, and
the first act of simply speaking with the other person does not
work, seek guidance from your priest on how to proceed. Be
careful, however, not to ask the priest to become a triangulated
referee. Instead, seek his counsel as a pastor.

5. *Remain open to feedback and try not to be defensive.* St.
Augustine wrote that God works in our lives through "exterior
admonition." Ann Garrido, author of *Redeeming Conflict*, points
out, "Conflict is a fertile field for 'exterior admonition'—sometimes overtly in others' words, many times just by what the situation itself seems to insinuate about us."[8] Exterior admonitions
often come as feedback from the person with whom we are in
conflict.

It is a significant deed of mercy, and a substantial exercise in
humility, to receive feedback about your role in a conflict from
the other person's perspective. It pains us to know that we have
hurt someone else or that our actions are not ideal. Garrido
notes that receiving feedback about ourselves is delicate because
it "lies at the intersection of two very basic human needs: the
need to learn and to grow, and the need to be loved and accepted
exactly where we are."[9] We bristle at feedback that suggests we
need to change something about ourselves or our behavior. This
can manifest as defensiveness or digging in our heels about our
position.

As a prayer of mercy, pray for the graces to receive feedback
with humility. Without humility, we risk escalating a conflict by

returning the feedback with something uncharitable. We also must pray for the graces to remain open to changing. Sometimes we shut down when we receive feedback. We say things such as "I'm not going to waste my time caring about what other people think of me. If they don't like me, too bad." While this attitude could reflect healthy self-esteem, balking at sincere feedback is not a helpful position to take when trying to resolve a genuine conflict in which you bear some responsibility. Instead, listen to what the other person says and ask questions to help you understand.

For example, upon speaking with the woman who interrupted me, she might have replied, "I know I interrupted, but I was just trying to help. You never accept my help!" If this had happened in real life, it would have revealed much about her intent. It also would have shown me a potential blind spot in my interactions—perhaps I did not accept her help. In listening to feedback, we may find that there is more to a conflict than we can perceive from our limited perspective.

6. *Do not gossip.* One of the most merciful deeds we can do to resolve conflict is to refrain from gossiping. Jesus said, "Go to your brother," not go tell it on the mountain! Gossip is verbal napalm that burns down reputations and interpersonal trust and goodwill without impunity. It leaves behind charred feelings and betrayed confidences, and it makes ashes out of good intentions. St. Faustina noted that if silence were strictly observed in her religious community, "there would not be any grumbling, bitterness, slandering, or gossip, and charity would not be tarnished. In a word, many wrongs would not be done."[10]

We can avoid gossip by going directly to our sister and refraining from talking about the resolution process and reconciliation. Gossip can be verbal, but it can also be digital. Do not post about interpersonal conflict or the resolution process on social media. When people resolve a conflict, they are vulnerable with each other. To recount the resolution publicly betrays trust and it creates a new conflict. Imagine how you would feel if you resolved a conflict with someone and apologized for your role. Later, you scroll Facebook and see the other person has posted, "So thankful for today. I received a long-overdue apology and feel so much better. #blessed."

7. *Seek understanding instead of relying on assumptions.* We are intuitive people and prone to make assumptions, but that does not mean that we have all the information to make *correct* assumptions. Instead of making assumptions, extend words of mercy by asking for clarity, try to give the other party the most generous interpretation, and remember that there is more to the story.

As a high school student, I volunteered as a candy striper at the local hospital. During my volunteer orientation, we watched a video that cautioned us about conversations in the hallway. In the video, two candy stripers look at a withering plant by a doorway, and one says, "He looks terrible. The nurse told me he's dying." The camera then shifts to reveal a young, healthy-looking patient with a cast on his leg, sitting in his hospital bed on the other side of the doorway. The man's face transitions from tranquility to terror because he assumes the candy stripers are talking about him. He made an incorrect assumption based on the limited data. In any situation, we only know part of the story. We may know what someone does or says, but we do not always know why.

8. *Ask for and grant forgiveness.* "While we were still sinners Christ died for us" (Rom 5:8). At a homily reflecting upon Hebrews 8:6–13, Pope Francis honed in on verses 12–13: "For I will forgive their evildoing and remember their sins no more. When he speaks of a 'new' covenant, he declares the first one obsolete. And what has become obsolete and has grown old is close to disappearing."

The Holy Father explained that "God always forgives! He never tires of forgiving. It is we who tire of asking for forgiveness.

But he never tires of forgiving."[11] God forgives entirely. As Isaiah records, "Though your sins be like scarlet, they may become white as snow; though they be red like crimson, they may become white as wool" (Is 1:18).

We have to muster the spiritual courage to ask for forgiveness when we wrong someone. Asking for forgiveness builds us in virtue, particularly in humility and charity. We must grant forgiveness generously, entirely, and unconditionally, as Christ does for us. Indeed, we must always forgive.

St. Faustina reminds us, "He who knows how to forgive prepares for himself many graces from God. As often as I look upon the cross, so often will I forgive with all my heart."[12]

9. *Seek the graces of Reconciliation.* If you can resolve a conflict, chances are you have learned areas where you need to grow or even areas where you fell short of charity, prudence, justice, or another virtue. When this is this case, in addition to seeking forgiveness from the person you have wronged, go to Reconciliation—literally get eyelash to eyelash with God again. We may never forget past conflict, and we may bear the scars, but Reconciliation helps us build something beautiful from the scar.

10. *Offer prayers of mercy.* Jesus told Faustina, "Through your prayers, you shall mediate between heaven and earth."[13] When we have a conflict, we can ask for God's mercy by praying for reconciliation between the people involved, for those with whom we are in conflict, and for our actions and words to be merciful. Faustina wrote that even during difficult times, "if we do not persevere in such prayer, we frustrate what the Lord wanted to do through us or within us."[14]

momentum builders

TIPS TO EXTEND PRAYERS OF MERCY

Here are three ways that you can extend prayers of mercy to get God's help when resolving conflict with someone in ministry:

Tip #1. Pray with your sister. Pray with the person with whom you are in conflict. A good prayer to say together is the Divine Mercy Chaplet.[15] When you meditate on Christ's passion and the depths of his mercies, the severity of a conflict may become significantly smaller. If you cannot pray with the person, pray *for her.*

Tip #2. Pray without ceasing. Even if it is difficult to pray, keep spending time with God. The greater your anguish, the greater the need for prayers of mercy. St. Faustina reminds us, "Let every soul remember these words: 'And being in anguish, He prayed longer.' I always prolong such prayer as much as in my power and in conformity with my duty."[16]

Tip #3. Pray for your own conversion. Rather than praying for the other person to see your side, to agree with you, or to alter their behavior, pray that all will receive the grace of the Holy Spirit and be converted to God's will. The conversion will inspire each person's will to be obedient to God's will. That will alleviate the conflict.

What If None of This Works?

Unfortunately, despite your best efforts, there may come a time when you feel you cannot resolve a conflict or reconcile with another person. Maybe the people involved are unwilling, or maybe hearts need more time to soften. There may exist a situation so abusive or so hostile that the people involved are unable to overcome the conflict. In women's ministry it is truly a sad day if Christian people, doing allegedly Christian work, cannot be reconciled. After all, we are supposed to work to help women grow in their relationship with Jesus.

If we cannot pull back the layers of conflict, grant forgiveness, and seek reconciliation to reclaim that mission, then it may be time to remember from Luke's gospel the fig tree that did not bear fruit. Jesus told the parable of a man who had a fig tree planted in his garden. When the man found the tree barren, he said to his gardener, "For three years now I have come in search of fruit on this fig tree but have found none. [So] cut it down. Why should it exhaust the soil?" (Lk 13:7–8). The gardener replied, "Sir, leave it for this year also, and I shall cultivate the ground around it and fertilize it; it may bear fruit in the future. If not you can cut it down" (Lk 13:8–9). Try your best to resolve conflict by fertilizing your relationship with the others involved by extending deeds, words, and prayers of mercy before walking away.

However, in Matthew's gospel, Jesus teaches that sometimes it is okay to walk away. The conditions of walking away, however, are that you do so in Christian charity and that you have done everything you can to resolve an issue. You must be in a place of consolation to discern whether to walk away. When Jesus commissioned the Twelve, he told them to go to the lost sheep of Israel:

> As you enter a house, wish it peace. If the house is worthy, let your peace come upon it; if not, let your peace return to you. Whoever will not receive you or listen to your words—go outside that house or town and shake the dust from your feet. (Mt 10:12–14)

If you walk away from a conflict or a relationship, shaking the dust emphasizes that our abilities to heal are finite. As we hear on Ash Wednesday, "Remember that you are dust, and to dust you shall return." What is dust is dead. The only one who can create something new from dust is God. If you walk away from a conflict, pray for God to mold the dust that you have left behind into something beautiful. I heard a priest say that even if you do shake the dust from your sandals, you are still leaving a bit of your truth behind. In time, there may still be reconciliation.

You may think that forgiveness and reconciliation are lofty goals and question whether this is actually possible. Let's face it—we live in a world that thrives on conflict. But yes, forgiveness and reconciliation are possible. I was able to witness a conflict between two women in ministry and their resolution. With their permission, I share their story as encouragement.

Veronica and Anne had a conflict about planning an event. Anne was a very gregarious, outgoing ministry leader. She always gathered many women around the table and had a leadership style that was directive in that she gave guidance but did not micromanage. She was also very affiliative, in that she wanted lots of people to have their hands in every endeavor.

Anne asked Veronica to plan an upcoming annual appreciation breakfast and to form a committee to help with the event. Veronica was a diligent and autonomous worker. She completed tasks with excellence and a cheerful heart. A natural introvert, however, Veronica did not enjoy working with large teams. She did not want to involve a committee because she was a busy mom, she worked full-time as a professional event planner, and she did not feel that she had time to facilitate a committee. Committees drained her energy.

Anne, however, was resolute that the breakfast needed to be planned through a committee. Anne wanted the event to unite a fractured women's ministry. Anne thought that if she had lots of stakeholders involved in the planning, the event would be unifying.

As the women discussed the issue, they made assumptions about the situation. Veronica assumed that Anne was using the committee to micromanage and that Anne did not trust her competence or respect her time. Meanwhile, Anne felt that Veronica was not being a team player and that she did not value unity in the group. Both women made assumptions based on incomplete information. Veronica had no idea that there was a fracture in the ministry or that Anne was trying to mend it. Anne had no idea that Veronica was a professional event planner or that she worked full-time.

One day Anne called Veronica and asked to have coffee with her. In effect she heeded Jesus' instruction to "go to your sister." Anne said, "I love that you are making so much progress on this event. The venue is beautiful, the menu is perfect, and I really like the speaker. But I have a question: Why aren't you using a committee like I asked? I feel like you are ignoring me." Veronica said, "I really don't have time to deal with a committee right now. I have a full-time job. I don't want to rally more people into something so simple. I'm a professional event planner, I can do this in my sleep. Why don't you just trust me?" Immediately Anne realized her incorrect assumption: Veronica was a team player. She was also fiercely competent and efficient.

Anne told Veronica, "Now I see. I did not know that you were an event planner. I know that you know what you are doing. But I still need you to make a committee." "Why?" Veronica asked, a little annoyed. Anne explained, "There were some hurt feelings about the last event, and I think that if we invite everyone to the table and listen to them, and involve them, it will heal hurt feelings." Being a new arrival to the ministry, Veronica was unaware that the event had some sad history. She told Anne that she was not interested in knowing the past details, then she said, "Okay. If having a committee is important to you, I will form one."

I learned of this story years later when Anne, Veronica, and I were having dinner together and chatting about how different we are but that we have always been able to work together. Anne and Veronica shared their story. As one of the people recruited to serve on the committee, I never detected a hint of conflict between the two women. During our meal, Anne told Veronica, "You know, Veronica, you showed real humility that day. I did not know what was going to happen." Veronica was a little incredulous and replied, "Even if I did not agree with you, I was going to do what you asked because I trust you." These women personify that "charity upholds and purifies our ability to love" and brings forward the fruits of joy, peace, and mercy (*CCC* 1827).

PONDER

Today's passage to ponder is Jesus' parable of the prodigal son, found in Luke 15:11–32.

> "A man had two sons, and the younger son said to his father, 'Father, give me the share of your estate that should come to me.' So the father divided the property between them. After a few days, the younger son collected all his belongings and set off to a distant country where he squandered his inheritance on a life of dissipation.
>
> "When he had freely spent everything, a severe famine struck that country, and he found himself in dire need. So he hired himself out to one of the local citizens who sent him to his farm to tend the swine. And he longed to eat his fill of the pods on which the swine fed, but nobody gave him any. Coming to his senses he thought, 'How many of my father's hired

workers have more than enough food to eat, but here am I, dying from hunger. I shall get up and go to my father and I shall say to him, "Father, I have sinned against heaven and against you. I no longer deserve to be called your son; treat me as you would treat one of your hired workers."'

"So he got up and went back to his father. While he was still a long way off, his father caught sight of him, and was filled with compassion. He ran to his son, embraced him and kissed him. His son said to him, 'Father, I have sinned against heaven and against you; I no longer deserve to be called your son.' But his father ordered his servants, 'Quickly bring the finest robe and put it on him; put a ring on his finger and sandals on his feet. Take the fattened calf and slaughter it. Then let us celebrate with a feast, because this son of mine was dead, and has come to life again; he was lost, and has been found.' Then the celebration began.

"Now the older son had been out in the field and, on his way back, as he neared the house, he heard the sound of music and dancing. He called one of the servants and asked what this might mean. The servant said to him, 'Your brother has returned and your father has slaughtered the fattened calf because he has him back safe and sound.' He became angry, and when he refused to enter the house, his father came out and pleaded with him. He said to his father in reply, 'Look, all these years I served you and not once did I disobey your orders; yet you never gave me even a young goat to feast on with my friends. But when your son returns who swallowed up your property with prostitutes, for him you slaughter the fattened calf.'

"[And the father] said to him, 'My son, you are here with me always; everything I have is yours. But now we must celebrate and rejoice, because your

brother was dead and has come to life again; he was
lost and has been found.'"

1. As you read this passage, think of a person with whom you
   have (or had) a significant conflict. Are you like the father,
   ever watching for the other person on the horizon? Do you
   see yourself as the son, needing to seek forgiveness?

2. If you have resolved this sort of deep rift, describe how you
   reached reconciliation. If you long to resolve this sort of rift,
   what is holding you back?

3. Reflecting upon your life, is there someone from whom
   you need to seek or grant forgiveness? How would seeking
   or granting forgiveness lighten your burden? How would
   forgiveness increase your peace and joy and that of your
   community?

4. Jesus told Faustina, "[S]peak of My mercy. Tell souls where
   they are to look for solace; that is, in the Tribunal of Mercy
   [sacramental confession]. There the greatest miracles take
   place [and] are incessantly repeated."[17] Think of the last time
   you went to Confession. Did you lay everything before Jesus?
   If so, how did you feel afterward? Share that feeling and what
   God has done for you through the sacrament. If this hasn't
   happened, what is holding you back?

5. This chapter presented ways to resolve conflicts with deeds,
   words, and prayers of mercy. What are some ways that you
   can extend mercy in women's ministry? How has a friend in
   ministry extended mercy to you?

Closing Prayer

Merciful Jesus, we know that you never tire of forgiving us. Please teach us to seek and accept your forgiveness. Help us to forgive others and to share deeds, words, and prayers of mercy. St. Faustina, pray for us. Amen.

8

Passing the Baton:

MENTORSHIP AND ACCOMPANIMENT

> Be not lax in celebrating. Be not
> lazy in the festive service of God.
> Be ablaze with enthusiasm. Let us
> be an alive, burning offering before
> the altar of God.
>
> —St. Hildegard of Bingen

SHARE

During one of the first women's ministry events I ever helped plan, our parish invited a Catholic author named Donna-Marie Cooper O'Boyle to speak at a mini-retreat about her book *The Domestic Church*, which our morning faith study had been reading. Our faith-study facilitator, Christina, led the effort to host the event, and several of us joined her.

As we prepared for the event, Christina showed us the ropes of hosting a parish event: how to put an announcement in the bulletin, request funds from the parish council, put an agreement in place with the speaker, reserve the room, and arrange for book sales. With this required preparatory work in hand, we set to the lively work of making personal invitations to all the women in the parish, not just the people who attended the faith study. Working on the team for this event taught me practical skills that helped prepare me to take the lead on planning another event several months later.

When the mini-retreat finally arrived, Donna-Marie spoke to our gathering about the dignity of women and our mission to mold our homes into what Pope John Paul II referred to as "domestic churches." When I met Donna-Marie, I had been interested in writing about my faith for most of my adult life but avoided *actually* writing by making excuses: I did not have time, I was too young, I was not smart enough, nobody would be interested in reading anything I wrote, or I might offend someone. The reality was that I did not have the confidence to write about my Christian faith, and I let my own brokenness get in the way of the Holy Spirit's nudges. Meeting Donna-Marie and listening to her share, with sincerity and simplicity, her journey as a Catholic woman, mom, and wife inspired me. After her presentation, I asked Donna-Marie if we could stay in touch, and we have been in touch ever since.

As I worked in women's ministries and started to form this book in my mind and heart, Donna-Marie continued to offer encouragement, ask about my progress, provide feedback, and point me to resources to help me refine ideas. She has grown to be a personal friend and mentor who has empowered me to respond to God's call to lead women closer to Christ.

APPLY
PRACTICAL MENTORSHIP AND SPIRITUAL ACCOMPANIMENT

My relationships with Christina and Donna-Marie exemplify two types of mentorship that are necessary in women's ministries: practical mentorship and spiritual mentorship.

Practical mentorship. Practical mentorship teaches skills, such as the ins and outs of how to plan and host events. If you are trying to start a new women's ministry group in your parish or take on a new role, you likely need practical mentorship—someone to teach you the necessary skills. If you cannot find that mentorship in your parish, get resourceful. Phone or email a friend. Call a parish where there is a women's ministry and ask one of the ministry leaders to teach you. Look online at women's ministry blogs for ideas. Start a thread in a social media group to ask questions. There are women out there who want to help you.

Spiritual accompaniment. The second type of mentorship is spiritual mentorship, or what the Synod of Bishops on Young People, the Faith and Vocational Discernment recently described as "accompaniment." This involves developing a significant relationship with another person, walking alongside on his or her faith journey through shared prayers, presence, conversation, and guidance.

Ministry leaders, whether new to this vocation or very experienced, also need spiritual accompaniment. Peer accompaniment can be especially valuable in ministry groups, which is where the Christian vocation comes to maturity. As the ministry group starts meeting, encourage women to practice peer accompaniment by meeting regularly, forming prayer partners, and hosting social functions in pairs or teams so that accompaniment happens naturally.

The bishops have also advised pastors to maintain a presence in group ministries to "guarantee suitable accompaniment."[1] Seek out sisters in ministry to accompany you, and ask the pastor for accompaniment.

Both practical mentoring and spiritual accompaniment are valuable and necessary in building a women's ministry. Let's first consider practical mentorship in-depth: its value and how to practice it in our ministry groups. Then we will turn our attention to spiritual accompaniment and how we can accompany each other in ministry and discipleship.

Getting Started: Practicing Practical Mentorship

A good mentor imparts knowledge, provides feedback, and invests time in relationship with the person being mentored. A good mentor gives the other person the autonomy to accept or reject feedback. However, the person receiving this advice recognizes the need for guidance and instruction, is receptive to feedback and coaching, and will put in the effort to learn new skills in order to eventually work independently of the mentor.

Practical mentorship is especially beneficial as we pass responsibilities to new ministry leaders or assume new responsibilities in a ministry. The entire ministry benefits when experience, expertise, and traditions are passed on from year to year.

The relationship between two people in a practical mentorship can be a close spiritual friendship, as we will consider later through the lives St. Hildegard of Bingen and Blessed Jutta of Disibodenberg, or it can be task specific. It is okay not to be spiritual besties with every person you teach or learn from in your community—that is just not practical!

Practical mentorship is important in any parish. Families frequently change parishes for a variety of reasons, and phases of life influence how involved someone can be in ministry leadership from year to year. It is important for leaders to prepare for those who will follow them by keeping careful records, maintaining continuity files (step-by-step directions for major initiatives and events), and offering practical mentorship. Without these things, basic knowledge—such as how to reserve a room or place an announcement in the bulletin—is easily lost, to the detriment of the next group of leaders. Without this kind of preparation, your successors may be forced to "reinvent the wheel" for standard processes. Or worse, they may experience hardship and stress due to a simple unfamiliarity with church policies and procedures, such as losing a meeting space because they failed to reserve a room in advance.

In addition to sharing tools and imparting knowledge, a good mentor gives others freedom to listen to the promptings of the Holy Spirit in their work and stretch their wings to offer their own charisms and creativity. When I took the lead on planning the parish mini-retreat, I followed the processes that Christina taught me and that our parish expected for events, but I added my own creative touches. For example, I invited a nun who taught liturgy at a nearby seminary to speak about the new Roman Missal. We moved the presentation from the parish library, which was our usual event location, into the church, where we practiced the new Mass responses together. Christina answered questions for me along the way, but she gave me room to lead, even if I did not do everything exactly as she would have.

When it was my turn to be the mentor for another woman who was taking the lead on the subsequent event, I gave her electronic continuity files and walked alongside her, letting her lead the way. The continuity files were in a digital folder, shared online, that contained copies of forms for funding, bulletin announcements, postcard invitations, schedules, speaker agreements, a post-event survey, and an after-action summary of what went well and ways to improve. In an age of cloud-based storage, sharing continuity files is an easy way for successive ministry teams to keep up the momentum!

How to Find (or Be) a Mentor

I often hear women say that they do not have good mentors. In fact, a 2018 CARA study on Catholic women at Georgetown University found that nearly 10 percent of Catholic women said that nobody has helped them understand what it means to be a woman in the Church.[2] That number should be zero!

Incorporate practical mentorship into ministry work so that women have the tools and know-how they need. Some ways to practice practical mentorship include:

1. *Ask for a mentor.* Our culture places huge emphasis on being independent, and while independence is a good thing, it sometimes dissuades us from asking for help. Being willing to learn is a gift, so don't be afraid to ask someone to teach you. Even if you want to do things yourself, consider mentorship as a way of inviting more experienced people to share their spiritual gifts of teaching, ministry, or exhortation. Pray for the humility to ask for mentorship. Just because you can do something independently does not mean it is best for the community.

2. *Work with teams.* If a team partners in ministry, there is breadth and depth of knowledge. People can become integral to the program, but a ministry's ability to hold a Bible study or event should never hinge on the skills or knowledge of one indispensable person. Recall Acts of Apostles: "All who believed were together and had all things in common" (Acts 2:44). That means sharing efforts in common, too.

3. *Consider online sources or events outside your parish to find mentorship.* Look to contemporary Catholic blogs, and drill down to see who published these posts—send those people emails to connect. Attend a women's ministry conference and talk to the organizers, the vendors, and the participants. Podcasts are a great way to find passive mentorship or accompaniment. Of course, digital resources break down at some point—our faith is incarnational; we are created to live in relationship with each other. However, digital resources can be a good starting place for information and sparking your creativity.

4. *Be a mentor by seeking opportunities to teach.* Look for opportunities to incorporate new people and teach them the ropes. No matter what your role in the ministry, seek out women

who could succeed you. Some people have an interest in ministry leadership and will naturally step up. Others need to be actively recruited because you see their gifts and potential.

5. *Be present.* Simply showing up can be an act of mentorship; you do not need to be in charge all the time. Being present communicates that you desire to participate with the community, that you value the efforts of others and have confidence in them, and that you are available. If you have experience with or a love for a given aspect of the ministry—say, coordinating a prayer group—let newer women know that you are willing to share your experience or offer guidance.

6. *Create continuity files and pass them on.* Continuity files provide a basic recipe. If someone follows the steps and uses the tools in a continuity file, she should be able to replicate the fundamentals of what has been done in the past. At the same time, this basic recipe leaves room for a person to add ingredients and flavors; use continuity files as a guide while adding new talents, resources, or ideas.

7. *Work for seamless transitions.* Plan for transitions in a leadership team, incorporating mentorship so that there is always a mix of experienced and new leadership on the team. On a team of six, for example, have four people rotate off the team, four new people join, and two stay in place to provide continuity and mentorship. Host a celebratory transitional meeting with the outgoing and incoming teams, so that there is space to learn from each other. Have a meal or reception to celebrate everyone's work and build relationships among the women.

8. *Be open to change.* As a mentor, you may feel very attached to certain aspects of the ministry. However, part of mentorship is giving others freedom to use their gifts and talents in the ways they feel called and equipped. Those we mentor may make different choices than we would make. It is normal to feel disappointment if this happens, but try to keep an open mind and heart.

9. *Resist the urge to manipulate or control.* Have you ever heard a mentor say something such as "If you do ____, I won't be involved." That is not mentoring; that is manipulating, and it creates a spirit of division. If you cannot be a mentor to someone, seek another way to serve with a joyful heart.

10. *The goal is discipleship.* The skills and how-tos of women's ministry are important, but good mentors remember that the work of ministry is to form disciples, not just to teach others to *do* all the things. Keep your eye on Jesus.

Practicing Spiritual Accompaniment

If practical mentorship is important in a ministry, accompaniment is critical. It involves prayerfully drawing near to someone in need of spiritual mentorship, walking with that person, asking questions, listening, guiding, offering instruction, and ultimately, through their own conversion, learning to accompany others. This process might look a lot like practical mentorship, but it is more.

My relationship with Donna-Marie has elements of practical mentorship; she offers guidance as we both pursue the craft of writing. However, her support has a deeply spiritual focus. Through conversations, prayers, tough questions, counsel, and patience, she accompanies me as a missionary disciple. She helps shine a light on God's nudges and helps me stay open to the promptings of the Holy Spirit.

We see this kind of spiritual mentorship in practice in the story of the road to Emmaus (see Luke 24:13–35). In the days following the crucifixion of Jesus and the subsequent reports of his resurrection, two men decided to leave their community in Jerusalem and set out for Emmaus, which was a town seven miles away. On their journey, they conversed about the events, and Jesus "drew near and walked with them" (Lk 24:15). Indeed, he *accompanied* them. Jesus started a conversation with the men by asking, "What are you discussing as you walk along?" (Lk 24:17). Gently, persistently, Jesus asked inviting questions, encouraging them to share their experience.

When the men described their belief that Jesus was a "prophet mighty in deed and word before God and all the people," they lamented, "But we were hoping that he would be the one to redeem Israel" (Lk 24:19, 21). In answering Jesus, they shared their hearts, their hopes, and disappointment. They expressed their amazement and even confusion that Jesus' body was missing from the tomb.

With understanding and affection, mixed with a slight rebuke, Jesus sparked their curiosity and facilitated their discernment by pointing them to their own scriptures: "Oh, how foolish you are! How slow of heart to believe all that the prophets spoke! Was it not necessary that the Messiah should suffer these things and enter into his glory?" (Lk 24:25). Then, beginning with Moses and all the prophets, Jesus interpreted the scriptures that referred to him. As accompanier, Jesus guided the men to understand, but he never told them what they needed to believe. Also, he never made his accompaniment conditional, because accompaniment is about steadfast love.

As the three approached Emmaus, Jesus gave the impression that he was going farther on, but the men urged him with an invitation: "Stay with us, for it is nearly evening and the day is almost over" (Lk 24:29). In this gesture, the accompanied invited further relationship with the accompanier. Jesus accepted their invitation and the conversation continued. When Jesus celebrated the first recorded Eucharist after the Resurrection, the men finally recognized him, but he vanished from their sight. With the zeal of conversion, the men felt compelled to return on the seven-mile trek to Jerusalem at once to proclaim the Good News. Like Mary Magdalene, they too became apostles to the apostles and shared prophetically what had been made known to them (see Luke 24:31–35).

At the Synod on Young People, the bishops identified this gospel story as a "paradigm of accompaniment" and noted that "the young are crying out for an authentic, radiant, transparent, joyful Church."[3] Of course, this desire for accompaniment is not limited to our youth; we are all crying out for the same thing! Our desire to live and serve an authentic, radiant, transparent, and joyful Church makes Emmaus-like accompaniment relevant for all.

To be accompanied, a person must be willing to allow someone else to "draw near." Or a person must be willing to invite someone to walk with her just like the men on the road to Emmaus invited Jesus to stay with them. The accompanied should welcome dialogue and have a willingness to wrestle with things that challenge her. She should desire holiness and seek to grow in discipleship. She must strive to be obedient to the promptings of the Holy Spirit. Just as the men in Emmaus went back to Jerusalem to accompany the community there, the accompanied, as she matures in her Christian vocation, should seek to accompany others.

St. Hildegard and Blessed Jutta, Models of Mentorship

St. Hildegard of Bingen and Blessed Jutta of Disibodenberg are both models and intercessors for mentorship and accompaniment. These women shared a kinship that started as practical mentorship and tutelage and grew to a spiritual accompaniment that helped to renew the medieval Church in Europe.

Hildegard was born into a noble German family in 1098. When she was eight, her parents placed her in the care of Jutta, an anchoress (a woman who had withdrawn from the world to pursue a life of prayers and contemplation) who had founded a monastery at Disibodenberg. Jutta mentored Hildegard in practical skills—gardening, weaving, spinning, and even the use of medicinal herbs. She also taught Hildegard how to read the Latin Bible and chant the Divine Office. Hildegard admired Jutta as a spiritual teacher and described that Jutta was "inundated with the grace of God, like a river flooded by many streams."[4]

When she was a teen and sufficiently mature, Hildegard entered the Disibodenberg monastery, and with the accompaniment of Jutta, she continued to study prayer, art, music, and work that characterized the Benedictine way. Hildegard was a mystic and prophet; she experienced God vividly through her senses and had visions. She confided her experiences to Jutta, and they accompanied each other as they grew spiritually.

In 1136, Jutta died and Hildegard became the prioress of the monastery. Hildegard's reputation for holiness spread and inspired women to join the community at Disibodenberg, which eventually outgrew the space available. In 1148, Hildegard and eighteen nuns left Disibodenberg and founded another community in Rupertsberg, and in short order, another community in Eibingen. As Hildegard's communities grew, she mentored and accompanied the nuns, but she also sought accompaniment from abbots, priests, and bishops.

At one point in her life, Hildegard discerned a prophetic call from God that commanded her to "say and write what you see and hear."[5] This call led Hildegard to compose her first book, *Scivias* (Know the Ways). However, Hildegard needed counsel to know that her call was from God and asked an abbot and the archbishop of Mainz to "draw near" and walk this stretch of road with her as she discerned the call. These men informed Pope Eugenius of her work and their impression that this was truly God's hand using Hildegard as his instrument. The pope joined in Hildegard's walk and sent her letters of encouragement. With the pope's encouragement and, indeed, his spiritual accompaniment, Hildegard proceeded to share the messages that God gave her. Hildegard's life was replete with relationships of mentorship and accompaniment. As one of the four women Doctors of the

Church, Hildegard can accompany us spiritually through the Communion of Saints. Ask for her intercession.

Using the Gift of Accompaniment

Like many of the ways in which the Holy Spirit prompts us to serve the Church, accompaniment is a charism. We must put in the work and be willing to accompany others, but we also must pray for the graces to be a good accompanier and to recognize who God calls us to accompany. Emmaus provides several characteristics of a good accompanier:

1. *A good accompanier must be well formed in the faith, prayerful, and on her own journey of growing in discipleship.* The Synod posited that a good accompanier should be balanced and understand her strengths as well as weaknesses and frailties, so that she can be accepting of those she accompanies.[6] Sometimes peers accompany each other and are formed together. Other times, an accompanier needs to be accompanied by her own spiritual guide or director, so that she, too, is growing in discipleship.

2. *A good accompanier goes out to meet the accompanied wherever they are and practices the ministry of simply being present.* Throughout the gospels, Jesus "draws near" to those in need of accompaniment (see John 4:1–42; Luke 24:13–35, 36–43). Jesus did not commission the Church to "stay where you are therefore and make disciples." Rather, the commission in Matthew 28:19 is to "*Go!*" The Holy Spirit may call you to accompany women who attend weekly Bible study at the parish, or you may be called to "draw near" to someone in a grocery-store checkout line, on the playground, or at work.

Accompaniment can begin anywhere! Too often I hear women say things such as "We had a table in the back of the church so that people could sign up for our Bible study, but nobody came." As a willing accompanier, do not wait behind a table for someone to come to you; take hold of the commission that Jesus gave the Church, climb over the pews or across the grocery-store checkout line, and go to them! Who is the Holy Spirit calling you to accompany?

3. *A good accompanier asks questions and listens patiently.* Good accompaniers ask questions to invite conversation. Through questions the accompanier learns about the accompanied, and gets to know their experiences, feelings, and struggles. A good accompanier must listen patiently to the accompanied. Pope Francis wrote that "listening, in communication, is an openness of heart which makes possible that closeness without which spiritual encounter cannot occur" (*Evangelii Gaudium* 171). In listening, accompaniers let the Holy Spirit work in their own hearts to increase empathy and sensitivity to the experience of others. Through listening, accompaniers also formulate new questions to help the accompanied, and they too can be molded by the Holy Spirit. Pray for the graces to be a patient listener. In listening we may perceive the Holy Spirit prompting us toward things we had not considered before.

As an accompanier, listen for questions around you. An invitation to accompany someone often comes in the form of a question from the accompanied. With Donna-Marie, my initial question was simple, "Can we keep in touch?"

4. *A good accompanier balances catechesis and correction with respect for an individual's freedom.* In listening, an accompanier often discerns ways to guide, assist, or instruct the accompanied. Just like a good mentor should not try to exercise control over a student, a good accompanier does not order the accompanied to take a particular action or condition a relationship on the accompanied doing certain things. Instead, an accompanier offers tools and catechesis for the accompanied. The accompanier may even offer fraternal correction.

St. Paul VI described this interaction between the accompanied and accompanier, in particular the conversation on the way to Emmaus, as a "dialogue of salvation" and added that we are "free to respond to it or reject it."[7] Freedom, offered the Synod, "is the essential condition of every life choice."[8] An accompanier knows that *true* freedom is intelligible and possible only in relation to truth (see John 8:31–32) and, above all, to charity (see 1 Corinthians 13:1–13; Galatians 5:13). As difficult as it may be, an accompanier offers catechesis and fraternal correction but must respect the freedom of the accompanied to move forward toward her own outcome.

As an accompanier, there can be a temptation to tell the accompanied what to do. If you are teaching a practical skill, by all means, teach the skill. But if you are accompanying someone in their spiritual growth, point them toward means of participating in their faith—point them to the sacraments; take them to Mass; direct them to scripture, Catholic books, and the writings of the saints. Offer fraternal correction, but respect the person's freedom. My friend Kelly has a true gift for respecting the freedom of the accompanied. She asks questions and listens, and points out things to consider, but her concluding question is always, "So what are you going to do?" She gives the individual the freedom to act as they discern.

5. *An effective accompanier serves joyfully.* An accompanier in a women's ministry often serves behind the scenes as a quiet force in the community, without taking center stage or seeking attention for themselves, "rejoicing in the fruits that the Spirit produces in those who open their hearts to him."[9]

In Emmaus, Jesus served the two men to help their formation. He could have easily gone back to Jerusalem to proclaim his own resurrection. Instead, he accompanied them in their conversion so that they could return to Jerusalem with the apostolic message that Jesus had indeed risen from the dead. Jesus did not take credit for any of this. In fact, he disappeared.

—momentum builders—

TIPS FOR MENTORING
WITH GRACE

Tip #1. Equip new leaders and help them feel supported. No one should ever have to reinvent the wheel or feel as if they do not have someone to turn to for guidance. With practical mentorship, teach the next group of leaders and pass along continuity files so that when you transition out of leadership roles, the incoming leaders are prepared to keep up the good work in the community. After training new leaders, let go and give the next team the freedom to bring their own strengths, personalities, and interests to the work.

Tip #2. Remember that the goal of accompaniment is spiritual formation. To be a good accompanier, you must strive toward closer relationship with God. When seeking accompaniment, look to women who are prayerful, show self-control, and are sound in faith, love, and endurance (see Titus 2:2).

Tip #3. Seek out opportunities to give and receive mentoring. Pursue relationships in which you have practical mentorship as both teacher and student (mentor and protégé), and spiritual mentorship as both accompanier and accompanied. In these four roles, you will build dynamism in your own growth as a women's ministry leader and disciple of Jesus. This dynamism will help renew your community.

Through teaching practical skills and spiritually accompanying sisters in Christ, we create an environment that can navigate and build upon the good work of the people who came before us. When outgoing leaders equip newcomers, and new leaders are willing to understand and accept instruction from their sisters in ministry, they foster seamless transitions and continuity in their work. Like Hildegard and Jutta, when we couple these practical transitions with spiritual mentorship, we can hope to build enduring women's ministries that lead women to Christ.

PONDER

Today's passage to ponder comes from Acts 8:26–39, the story of Philip accompanying the Ethiopian on the road to Gaza.

> Then the angel of the Lord spoke to Philip, "Get up and head south on the road that goes down from Jerusalem to Gaza, the desert route." So he got up and set out. Now there was an Ethiopian eunuch, a court official of the Candace, that is, the queen of the Ethiopians, in charge of her entire treasury, who had come to Jerusalem to worship, and was returning home. Seated in his chariot, he was reading the prophet Isaiah. The Spirit said to Philip, "Go and join up with that chariot." Philip ran up and heard him reading Isaiah the prophet and said, "Do you understand what you are reading?" He replied, "How can I, unless someone instructs me?" So he invited Philip to get in and sit with him. This was the scripture passage he was reading:
>
> "Like a sheep he was led to the slaughter,
> and as a lamb before its shearer is silent,
> so he opened not his mouth.
> In (his) humiliation justice was denied him.
> Who will tell of his posterity?
> For his life is taken from the earth."

> Then the eunuch said to Philip in reply, "I beg you, about whom is the prophet saying this? About himself, or about someone else?" Then Philip opened his mouth and, beginning with this scripture passage, he proclaimed Jesus to him. As they traveled along the road they came to some water, and the eunuch said, "Look, there is water. What is to prevent my being baptized?" Then he ordered the chariot to stop, and Philip and the eunuch both went down into the water, and he baptized him. When they came out of the water, the Spirit of the Lord snatched Philip away, and the eunuch saw him no more, but continued on his way rejoicing.

1. As you read this passage slowly and carefully, consider how this encounter mirrors the accompaniment between Jesus and the men on the road to Emmaus (see Luke 24:13–35).
2. Write down the names of people who have mentored or accompanied you. Which of these people had the greatest role in forming who you are today? Give thanks to God for all the ways these people have nurtured you.
3. Think about a time you experienced a transition in leadership roles (either within or outside of ministry). What were some practices that helped the transition? How might practical mentorship have aided the transition?
4. Are there people currently in your community to whom you could be a practical mentor? List them. Now select one person and consider how you
   - seek opportunities to provide practical mentorship to that person,
   - hear the person asking for mentorship,
   - are present for that person,
   - work with a team to offer mentorship,
   - create continuity files and pass them on,
   - facilitate transitions in ministry for this person,

- give true mentorship without manipulating, and
- keep your eye on discipleship.
5. Think about someone with whom you share an accompanying relationship. Consider how you
   - seek continuous formation to be a good accompanier,
   - draw near to each other,
   - ask questions and listen patiently,
   - balance catechesis and correction with respect for an individual's freedom, and
   - serve each other joyfully.

Closing Prayer

Lord Jesus, in journeying on the Emmaus roads of life, we travel with our sisters in Christ. Especially during transitions, help us be mentors and accept mentorship for the betterment of our communities. Give us the desire and grace to be good accompaniers and to seek accompaniment as did St. Hildegard and Blessed Jutta. May we, like Mary Magdalene, St. Peter, and the men on the road to Emmaus, be witnesses to your resurrection. May we be ever aware that you are at our side as we joyously proclaim you as Lord. Amen.

Conclusion

A few years ago, I spoke at a women's retreat in the Netherlands. After the retreat's end, I imposed upon my mother-in-law's generous childcare for an extra day, and my friend Michelle and I made an overnight pilgrimage to Paris before flying home. The Cathedral of Notre Dame on Ile de la Cité and the shrines of St. Catherine Labouré and St. Vincent de Paul on Rue du Bac beckoned us.

With an economy rental car and a fifty-eight-euro reservation at a hostel called Hotel Dieu, we set out for Paris. We selected Hotel Dieu as our hostel because if you are looking at the front of the Cathedral of Notre Dame, Hotel Dieu is exactly to your left. No matter where we wandered in Paris, we knew we could find our way back to Our Lady's Cathedral.

Like the men who encountered Christ on the road to Emmaus, and like all earnest pilgrims, we never could have anticipated the ways that we would encounter Christ in magnificent Paris. As I maneuvered our manual-transmission car toward the city, we brimmed with excitement, as Parisians on mopeds weaved in and out of traffic, testing my most seasoned Washington, DC, driving skills. By the time we arrived at Notre Dame, my clutch foot trembled with fatigue from the syncopated dance of stopping and starting, downshifting and upshifting. After parking in an inconspicuous garage underneath the cathedral, we gathered our American-sized luggage and squeezed into a miniscule, European-sized elevator that took us from the garage onto the mall above. Pulling our clunky suitcases into the lobby of Hotel Dieu, we learned that Hotel Dieu is an active hospital. In fact, it is the oldest hospital in Paris and has been in operation since AD 651. Yes, that's right, AD 651—nearly one thousand years older than the first permanent settlement in the New World.

The hospital admissions clerk greeted us and understood that we were checking into the hostel, not the hospital, and directed us to the sixth floor, where amid signs for anesthesia and radiology we found the sparse but tidy Hotel Dieu. A kind Parisian woman welcomed us and led us to our room, where we flopped onto our twin beds and looked up at the ceiling, which contained a skylight with a retractable window. I climbed onto a chair and stuck my head through the skylight to admire the rooftops. At that moment, and as if right on cue, the bells of Notre Dame peeled, welcoming us to Our Lady's church. *Bienvenue à Paris!*

After a brief rest, Michelle and I eagerly walked to the Rue du Bac to visit the shrines of the saints Catherine Labouré and Vincent de Paul. Along the way we admired Parisian perfumes and the buttery aroma of breads and croissants wafting out of the bakeries.

Our first stop was the Shrine of St. Catherine Labouré. The Blessed Mother appeared to Catherine at this location in 1830, directing her to have forged what we now call the Miraculous Medal. The medal depicts Mary holding a round orb with a cross on top. Mary wears rings of precious stones on her hands, and rays of light pour from her fingers. The rays are symbols of the graces that Our Lady spreads out to the people who ask her. The prayer "Oh Mary, conceived without sin, pray for us who have recourse to thee" is scrawled in an oval arc across the top half of the medal. The flip side of the medal displays a cross and initial "M" for Mary and contains images of the Sacred Heart of Jesus and Immaculate Heart of Mary. Starting in 1832, the medal was given out on the streets of Paris with instruction to "pray for miracles." Hence, the title "the Miraculous Medal."

When we arrived at the shrine, a Spanish Mass was in progress. We recognized the Eucharistic Prayers and joined our English prayers to those of the Spanish pilgrims. Since we were quite late to Mass, we were not planning to receive Communion. However, as other pilgrims lined up for Communion, the Spanish-speaking usher shuffled me toward the Communion line. In Spanish, I asked, "Can I still go?" He responded, "*¿Ha confesado?*" which means "Have you confessed?" Indeed, I had. I went to Confession at the retreat the day before. I nodded, "*Sí.*" To which he responded, "*¿Pues?*" which means "Well then?" and he ushered us to the front of the church. Though woefully late to Mass, I scooted up the Communion line and received the Eucharist in front of the uncorrupt body of Catherine Labouré.

After Mass we prayed before St. Catherine and placed our written prayer petitions within a basket of other pilgrims' petitions. We then made our way down the block to the Shrine of St. Vincent de Paul, where another Mass was in progress. This time we recognized the inflection and tone of the language as Polish and the prayers as the *Angus Dei*. St. Vincent's uncorrupt body is kept enclosed in glass above the main altar. By this point in the liturgy, a thick cloud of incense hung heavily around St. Vincent's body, creating a powerful visual of heaven and earth uniting in the eucharistic banquet.

We participated in the eucharistic liturgy, again joining our English prayers with the voices of the other pilgrims. As the faithful lined up for Communion, we joined the movement toward the altar with arms crossed over our chests, as a non-verbal, universal symbol that a person is presenting herself for a blessing but not to receive the Eucharist—or so we thought.

As we stood in front of the priests, we bowed, with arms crossed over our chests, reverencing the host. However, as we straightened our postures, the priests said in unison, "*Corpus Christi.*" Reflexively, we said, "Amen," as the priests moved the hosts toward our mouths and we received Communion again.

With wide eyes and surprised expressions, we returned to our pew for the conclusion of the liturgy. We had not intended to receive. We were tardy, jabbering, enthusiastic American pilgrims who wandered our way into a Polish Mass in a Parisian church, and yet, like men on the Road to Emmaus, and the early disciples in the community of Acts 2:42, God chose us to make himself known to us in the breaking of the bread.

God persistently chose us on our pilgrimage. We learned later that *Hotel Dieu* means "hostel of God" and that it had its origins as a Catholic hospital for the poor. From placing us in hospital beds on the steps of his mother's cathedral, leading us to Mass at St. Catherine's shrine, and encountering him again at another Mass with Polish pilgrims, God chose us. We just showed up, recognized him, and were joyful in the experiences!

And God chooses you! You, dear reader, who picked up this book with initial curiosity. God chooses you and seeks you. Do you know the gift of God? Do you want to share the joy of that gift with others? God placed you where you are, at this very moment, because God is beckoning you on this pilgrimage to walk with him.

We have covered a lot of ground in the past eight chapters. We started this adventure with a conversation about the blessing of spiritual friends with St. Teresa of Ávila and how to partner with other women as we embark on ministry work. Then we transitioned to considering what our vocation is and how a vocation to women's ministry is a "call within a call." We also explored how we can enter into prayerfully discerning our vocation with spiritual friends and with St. Teresa of Calcutta as our guide. Through discernment God will give us certainty, peace, and joy.

From there, we explored how God gives us the graces of charisms, and that we are to serve him with these spiritual gifts. With foundational friendships and discernment of our vocation and spiritual gifts, we considered that our service in ministry begins with an invitation that is received with hope and progresses with relationships of hospitality, with St. Elizabeth Ann Seton as our guide.

As women's ministry leaders, we explored how to stay mindful of reaching out to others, getting outside of our comfort zones, and listening to the "we shoulds" in our communities. Through reaching out, we share the joy of the Gospel with those who, like the woman at the well, did not know the gift of God.

As women's ministries expand and build traditions, we considered how healthy pruning done in love and with consistent assessment helps to improve our practices. Then, recognizing our limited human condition, we acknowledged that we sometimes fall short of love that God calls us to offer our sisters in Christ. When this happens, we must resolve conflict with mercy, grant forgiveness, and ask for forgiveness. We pray that reconciliation and a spirit of cooperation will mold our communities so that we can continue to build the Church with joy!

Finally, knowing that each of us has an exit from our current roles in ministry, we learned that through practical mentorship, we can pass on institutional knowledge and continuity to keep the momentum during ministry transitions. We also joined Jesus on the road to Emmaus to understand that we are called to be accompanied by friends in ministry and to accompany others so that we grow in faith. Through accompaniment, we come to recognize Jesus—his presence, his calling, and his abundant blessings.

My prayer for you is that this book has inspired holy conversations about building spirited, joyful, evangelistic women's ministries. I hope that as Michelle and I received blessing after unexpected blessing, you too will have the eyes to see God blessing your work and making himself known to you on your path. As you walk forward in ministry, I pray that you harness the joyful energy of the visitation and let it propel you forward as you reach out and share the Gospel. As you move forward in your ministries, remember St. Teresa of Calcutta's words: "Joy is prayer. Joy is strength. Joy is love. Joy is a net of love by which we catch souls."[1] Harness that joyful momentum.

Acknowledgments

This book came to be thanks to God's promptings in a "light silent sound" (1 Kgs 19:12) and through the steadfast encouragement of tremendous friends and mentors.

For their support for this project, I thank Stephanie Sibal, Emily Wichland, and the entire Ave Maria Press team. I am grateful to my editor and friend Heidi Hess Saxton for sharing a conversation about this book idea in Lancaster, Pennsylvania, in 2018, and for her feedback and keen editorial eye throughout the writing process.

Archbishop Timothy Broglio of the Archdiocese for the Military Services, USA, has made my work with the Military Council of Catholic Women possible. He took this ministry under his wing in 2012 and has generously shepherded us and reminded us always *quaerite regnum dei*: seek God's kingdom. Archbishop, for your care, guidance, and trust in me, I am profoundly grateful. Bishop Neal Buckon, whether celebrating Mass in the San Diego Mission, or singing old Army songs in a ballroom in Chattanooga, I admire your diligence and am grateful for your pastoral care. To the Good Fr. Joe Deichert, if I offer any good counsel in these pages, it is because of your counsel; you are a shepherd among shepherds. Monsignor Brian Donahue and Fr. Redmond Raux, you have walked with me since I became an Army wife. You are honest, generous, corrective, and insightful. Thank you for guiding me. My words of thanks will always fall short of the depth of gratitude and love I feel toward this Archdiocese and her clergy, so I offer my prayers for you all and trust that the Holy Spirit will perfect them.

To the Military Council of Catholic Women: You ladies are my soul sisters. You support me, teach me, love me, laugh and cry with me, encourage me, and help me to keep pressing forward when life gets tough. You inspired this book from its inception and continue to see it through. There are too many beautiful sisters in Christ to name, but I would be remiss not to acknowledge my steadfast MCCW sisters: Erin Raymond, Erin Lunday, Nancy Belmont, Marisol Morales, Marcia Stokes, Lisa Miklos, Michelle Hokenson, Loretta Endres, and Lynda MacFarland.

For the current MCCW leaders who have been so supportive of this project, I thank especially Kim Miller. You are a wonderful leader for this ministry. I'm glad to be part of the Kimberbeth duo and glad for your friendship. Team Grace: Denise Hummel, Joan LaPore, Bernadette Kovalsick, Aly Tugaoen, Bevin Landrum, Anni Harry, Jean Dery, Linda Coleman, Brenda Nonnweiler, and Eleanor Gentilini, may we always "be strengthened by the grace that is in Christ Jesus" (2 Tim 2:1). Sue Parker, thanks for keeping it real and for your bee-utiful soul.

Several friends in Christ have particularly lifted me along the way. Melissa Luria, I love that we have grown up in our faith together. To my extroverted friend Nicole Burns, thank you for adopting this introvert. Kelly Oliver, "Iron is sharpened by iron; one person sharpens another" (Prv 27:17). You are that iron for me. Dollia Lemus, thank you for your friendship and "little way" spirituality. Karen Fletcher, when I showed you the completed draft of this book, you put your hands on it and prayed for my words and for all future readers. Thank you for your prayerful presence always. Julie and Kurt Carrick, thank you for the blessed book conversations and for joining my family's prayers to yours. Beth Manning, you are the Popcorn to my Awesome Sauce. Maggie Bourne, your generous heart is unparalleled, and whether road-tripping across the El Paso desert or the French countryside, I'm fortunate that you adventure with me!

I am thankful for the mentorship and friendship of Donna-Marie Cooper O'Boyle. Thank you for encouraging me to write this book at West Point in 2011, for your feedback as I worked through chapters, and for chasing steeples with me!

My children—Patrick, Hannah, and George—you are my greatest joy in life. Thank you for your encouragement. Hannah, thank you for letting me read portions of this book aloud to you and for your feedback. I pray daily for your Catholic faith and God's blessings for you. To my mother-in-law, Donna Tomlin: Mom, thank you for helping me balance kids, work, and life. As a fellow Army wife, you walked similar challenges and joys and know that with God and Our Lady's intercession, all things are possible.

Gregory, you are home and my best friend. This book would not have happened without you. You cared for our family while I spent evenings and weekends writing, you read and provided helpful critique for every chapter, and you encouraged me to keep going when I felt frustrated. I love you; you are the real superstar.

Notes

Introduction: They Shared All Things in Common

1. For more information on the Military Council of Catholic Women, visit www.mccw.org.

2. John Paul II, *Letter of John Paul II to Women*, June 29, 1995, https:// w2.vatican.va/content/john-paul-ii/en/letters/1995/documents/hf_jp-ii_ let_29061995_women.html.

3. Teresa of Ávila, *The Interior Castle*, trans. Mirabai Starr (New York: Riverhead Books, 2003), 38.

4. Teresa of Ávila, *Interior Castle*, 38.

1. Foundational Relationships: The Favor of Spiritual Friendship

1. Karol Wojtyla, *Love and Responsibility* (San Francisco: Ignatius Press, 1993), 89.

2. Wojtyla, *Love and Responsibility*, 89–90.

3. Teresa of Ávila, *The Collected Works of St. Teresa of Ávila*, trans. Kieran Kavanaugh and Otilio Rodriguez, vol. 2 (Washington, DC: ICS Publications, 1980), 67.

4. Teresa of Ávila, 66–67.

5. Colleen Duggan, *Good Enough Is Good Enough: Confessions of an Imperfect Catholic Mom* (Notre Dame, IN: Ave Maria Press), xvii.

6. Hans Urs von Balthasar, *The Glory of the Lord: A Theological Aesthetics*, vol. 1, *Seeing the Form* (Edinburgh: T&T Clark, 1982), 18.

7. Mark M. Gray and Mary L. Gauthier, *Catholic Women in the United States: Beliefs, Practices, Experiences, and Attitudes* (Washington, DC: Center for Applied Research in the Apostolate, 2018), https://cara.georgetown.edu/ CatholicWomenStudy.pdf.

8. This instruction is found in *Code of Canon Law*, c. 510, sec. 3, c. 777, sec. 5, in *Code of Canon Law Latin-English Edition* (Washington, DC: Canon Law Society of America, 1999).

9. *Code of Canon Law*, c. 773.

10. Teresa of Calcutta, *Mother Teresa: Come Be My Light*, ed. Brian Kolodiejchuk (New York: Doubleday, 2007), 78.

2. A Call within a Call: Discerning a Vocation to Women's Ministry

1. Mark E. Thibodeaux, *God's Voice Within: The Ignatian Way to Discover God's Will* (Chicago: Loyola Press, 2010), 12, Kindle.

2. Congregation for the Clergy, *General Directory for Catechesis*, sec. 231, http://www.vatican.va/roman_curia/congregations/cclergy/documents/rc_con_ccatheduc_doc_17041998_directory-for-catechesis_en.html.

3. Ignatius of Loyola, *The Spiritual Exercises of Saint Ignatius*, trans. George E. Ganss (Chicago: Loyola Press, 1992), para. 13, 316.

4. Ignatius of Loyola, *Spiritual Exercises*, para. 317.

5. These attitudes come from Warren Sazama, "Some Ignatian Principles for Making Prayerful Decisions," Marquette University (website), accessed April 6, 2019, https://www.marquette.edu/faith/ignatian-principles-for-making-decisions.php.

6. See Ignatius of Loyola, *Spiritual Exercises*, para. 5.

7. Ignatius of Loyola, para. 169.

8. Teresa of Calcutta, *Mother Teresa: Come Be My Light*, ed. Brian Kolodiejchuk (New York: Doubleday, 2007), 14.

9. Teresa of Calcutta, *Mother Teresa: Come Be My Light*, 14.

10. Teresa of Calcutta, 14.

11. Teresa of Calcutta, 40.

12. Teresa of Calcutta, 41.

13. Teresa of Calcutta, *Mother Teresa: In My Own Words*, ed. Jose Luis González-Balado (Liguori, MO: Liguori Publications, 1997), 78.

14. Teresa of Calcutta, *Mother Teresa: In My Own Words*, 19.

3. United in Hope: Cultivating Christian Hospitality

1. Catherine O'Donnell, *Elizabeth Seton: American Saint* (Ithaca, NY: Cornell University Press, 2018), 119.

2. O'Donnell, *Elizabeth Seton*, 114.

3. O'Donnell, 122.

4. O'Donnell, 118, 121.

5. O'Donnell, 137.

6. "Holy Quotes from Mother Teresa," *Franciscan Spirit*, September 3, 2018, https://blog.franciscanmedia.org/franciscan-spirit/holy-quotes-from-mother-teresa.

4. Gifted to Serve: Offering Our Charisms

1. St. Thomas Aquinas taught that since God alone is not a created being, God is the only one who can work miracles by his own power.

2. See John Paul II, "Papal Homily at Holy Mass with the Bishop and Priests of the Diocese of Acosta," Vatican website, July 22, 2000, http://w2.vatican.va/content/john-paul-ii/en/homilies/2000/documents/hf_jp-ii_hom_20000722_les-combes.html.

3. See *Code of Canon Law*, c. 519.

4. Thérèse of Lisieux, *The Story of a Soul* (Charlotte, NC: Tan Classics, 2010), 4.

5. John Paul II, *Letter to Women*, Vatican website, June 29, 1995, https://w2.vatican.va/content/john-paul-ii/en/letters/1995/documents/hf_jp-ii_let_29061995_women.html.

6. Thérèse of Lisieux, *Story of a Soul*, 4.

7. It is a good idea to have written duty descriptions because defined roles keep women from stepping on one another's toes, they carve out opportunities for everyone to serve, and they create clear expectations of what each job entails, so that women can make informed decisions about their calling, competence, and commitment to take on specific roles.

8. Thérèse of Lisieux, *Story of a Soul*, 4.

5. Go to the Well: "Inreach" and Outreach

1. Cheryl C. D. Hughes, *Katharine Drexel: The Riches-to-Rags Life Story of an American Catholic Saint* (Grand Rapids, MI: William B. Eerdmans, 2014) 245–46, Kindle.

2. "Saint Katharine Drexel," *Franciscan Media*, accessed April 6, 2019, https://www.franciscanmedia.org/saint-katharine-drexel.

3. See Hughes, *Katharine Drexel*, 4034.

6. Return to Draw Water: Practicing Assessment

1. http://www.katharinedrexel.org/sisters-of-the-blessed-sacrament/social-justice/?doing_wp_cron=1566165322.0588500499725341796875.

2. A printable resource with the full novena is available at http://www.katharinedrexel.org/wp-content/uploads/2014/04/printable-novena.pdf.

7. Go to Your Sister: Resolve Conflict with Mercy

1. See Ann M. Garrido, *Redeeming Conflict: 12 Habits for Christian Leaders* (Notre Dame, IN: Ave Maria Press 2016), 12–13.

2. See Garrido, *Redeeming Conflict*, 13.

3. Francis, *When God Forgets*, Libreria Editrice Vaticana, January 23, 2015, https://w2.vatican.va/content/francesco/en/cotidie/2015/documents/papa-francesco-cotidie_20150123_when-god-forgets.html.

4. Mary Faustina Kowalska, *Diary: Divine Mercy of My Soul*, 3rd ed. (Stockbridge, MA: Marian Press, 1987), 742. All citations of the *Diary* refer to this edition.

5. Kowalska, *Diary*, para. 1158.

6. Kowalska, para. 1165.

7. Ewa Czaczkowska, *Faustina: The Mystic and Her Message* (Stockbridge, MA: Marian, 2014), 301.

8. Garrido, *Redeeming Conflict*, 136.

9. Garrido, 137.

10. Kowalska, *Diary*, para. 552.

11. Francis, *When God Forgets*.

12. Kowalska, *Diary*, para. 390.

13. Kowalska, para. 438.

14. Kowalska, para. 872.

15. Many online resources are available to help you, including this one here: https://www.thedivinemercy.org/assets/pdf/momm/worksheets/How_to_Recite_the_Chaplet_D_K2-HS.pdf.

16. Kowalska, *Diary*, para. 872.

17. Kowalska, para. 1448.

8. Passing the Baton: Mentorship and Accompaniment

1. *Final Document of the Synod of Bishops: Young People, the Faith and Vocation Discernment*, para. 96, accessed April 6, 2019, http://www.synod2018.va/content/synod2018/en/fede-discernimento-vocazione/final-document-of-the-synod-of-bishops-on-young-people--faith-an.html.

2. Mark M. Gray and Mary L. Gauthier, *Catholic Women in the United States: Beliefs, Practices, Experiences, and Attitudes* (Washington, DC: Center for the Applied Research in the Apostolate, 2018), https://cara.georgetown.edu/CatholicWomenStudy.pdf.

3. *Final Document of the Synod of Bishops*, para. 166.

4. Gloria Durka, *Praying with Hildegard of Bingen* (Winona, MN: Christian Brothers Press, 1991), 37.

5. Durka, *Praying with Hildegard*, 21.
6. See *Final Document of the Synod of Bishops*, para. 102.
7. *Final Document of the Synod of Bishops*, para. 75.
8. *Final Document of the Synod of Bishops*, para. 72.
9. *Final Document of the Synod of Bishops*, para. 102.

Conclusion

1. "Holy Quotes from Mother Teresa," *Franciscan Spirit*, September 3, 2018, https://blog.franciscanmedia.org/franciscan-spirit/holy-quotes-from-mother-teresa.

ELIZABETH TOMLIN is a Catholic author, general counsel for the Archdiocese of the Military Services, USA, and a catechist and director of stewardship for the Military Council of Catholic Women, where she also served as president, director of faith formation, and finance manager.

Tomlin earned her bachelor of science degree in chemistry from the College of William and Mary in 2002 and her juris doctor from the George Mason University School of Law in 2010. She is a member of the New York State Bar, Catholic Bar Association, John Carroll Society, Catholic Women of the Chapel, and the Military Spouse JD Network.

Tomlin is a regular contributor to *Salute*, the magazine of the Archdiocese of Military Services, and *The Well*, the newsletter of the Military Council of Catholic Women. She has twice been a speaker at the Mid-Atlantic Congress and occasionally writes for WINE: Women In the New Evangelization and CatholicMom.com.

She lives with her husband, Gregory, and their children in Washington.

Joyfulmomentum.org
Facebook: joyfulmomentum
Instagram: @elizabethannetomlin